Thank you for
caring.

signature

Leonarda Quispe Vargas is 6 years old and works and lives in the highland region of Apolobamba, Bolivia, where she helps her siblings care for the family's llamas and alpacas.

It is a job that exposes her to cold, wind, and sun and makes it difficult for her to attend school. Nevertheless, a job, not at all uncommon for some of the world's poor.

LIVING ON A DOLLAR A DAY

THE LIVES AND FACES OF THE WORLD'S POOR

THOMAS A. NAZARIO

Photographs by Renée C. Byer

I dedicate this book, first, to all those around the world who have so little, who work so hard, and who, in spite of all the difficulties they face in life, continue to care for all those they know and love. And second, to my mother, Rachel Pascual, who throughout every day of my life and in at least one of many different ways let me know that she loved me, as well as my wife, Erica, my son Bryan and my daughter Lauren for being, above all, my best friends. — *Thomas A. Nazario*

The Forgotten International
theforgottonintl.org

The Quantuck Lane Press

Contents

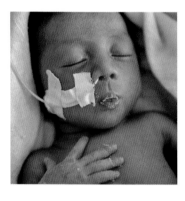

Foreword

The Dalai Lama

While situations and surroundings are different, people everywhere are more the same than different. All human beings, from the very rich to the very poor, anywhere in the world, all wish to be happy and to avoid suffering. Unfortunately, more than one billion of the world's people live in extreme poverty, defined by the World Bank as those who live on less than $1.25 per day.

The inequity among people in the world is very extreme. It can be the product of the struggle to survive in an inhospitable environment, it can be the result of a government system which does not provide its people with necessary services, or it can simply be the outcome of a family losing its main breadwinner. While some people possess more wealth, more good fortune, and more resources than they can ever use, so many others lack even the basic necessities of life. This great unfairness in the human condition can only be remedied when people everywhere care about economic injustice and feel the moral obligation to help those less fortunate than themselves.

This book, *Living on a Dollar a Day,* shows images of women, children, and families in our global community who suffer every day from the effects of extreme poverty. Their stories tell us that they have the same hopes and dreams for themselves and for their children as anyone else in the world. However, circumstances often outside of their control, such as changing climate, military conflict, political oppression, or the lack of access to basic health care and education, prevent this realization.

With their book, The Forgotten International offers two important means of alleviating poverty and reaching toward economic justice. First, to bring awareness of the problem of extreme poverty and show what it means in the daily lives of people in different parts of the world and, second, to offer the knowledge of how to help. The list of organizations found in this book offers everyone the opportunity to take action, big or small, to help those less fortunate.

Professor Thomas Nazario and his organization, The Forgotten International, strive to make a difference in the lives of others and to help alleviate the misery of the poorest of the poor. I wish them success in their noble work.

Introduction

I guess it can be argued that the inspiration behind the making of this book first came into being when I was about four years old and growing up in and around Spanish Harlem on the island of Manhattan in New York City. My mother, a recent arrival from Cuba, was a seamstress who, at the time, occasionally got odd jobs in a variety of sewing factories in lower Manhattan. My dad, who was born in Puerto Rico and met my mother while stationed near Guantánamo base in Cuba, came to New York with my mother and worked as an auto mechanic for a number of years while I was growing up. My parents, of course, had little

money. My mother would go to the market every day, buy what she needed, and make my brother and me rice and beans. It's how we got by from day to day and it seemed we always had enough money. In addition to the rice and beans my mother would always find the money to serve us some chicken or meat, hence, my brother and I always felt that we were pretty well off. It wasn't until I was four that I began to get a better sense of how well off we were.

Once a year our family would go out to dinner. It was a way my father had of simply doing something different and thanking my mother for always preparing our family's meals. The thinking was that everyone deserved at least one day off and that one day was Thanksgiving. It seemed that a restaurant not too far from where we lived always had a Thanksgiving Day special. The restaurant, then called Howard Johnson's served dinner for a family of four for about seven dollars. This was in the mid-1950s and this amount of money today would hardly buy you a sandwich let alone a family dinner. Nevertheless, when I was four and on one such Thanksgiving Day while driving to the restaurant I looked out of the side window of our car and noticed a woman and a small child, even smaller than myself, going through a garbage can, apparently looking for their dinner. Even at my age, I had seen this kind of thing before, but never involving a mother and a child and never on Thanksgiving Day.

It seemed so unfair, so cruel, and so sad, almost like the city had forgotten her and her child on Thanksgiving. And it was at that point that I decided there must be something wrong in the world to allow this to happen and that the world was not as fair as I had thought. By the time I had gotten home that evening, after eating my turkey dinner, which came with a slice of apple pie à la mode, I decided that when I grew up I would like to do something to help relieve some of the unfairness that existed outside my apartment door, and since then the image of the woman and her child going through the garbage has remained with me.

As I grew older and began to attend the public schools in and around the city of New York, I began to notice too that some kids came to school knowing far more than others. They had books at home, parents who stressed education, and dreams about becoming a doctor, lawyer, or Indian chief upon graduation and entering the world. I, on the other hand, came from a different socioeconomic culture and never thought about schooling or what school might bring. Instead, I was quite good at stickball, loved to hang out with my buddies, and occasionally got a crush on a girl or two but never had the courage to approach them.

Luckily, one day, one of those girls who I loved from afar asked me a question that changed my life forever. She said, "Hey Tom, what college are you going to?" Again, few Puerto Rican kids who grew up in inner-city New York ever thought about higher education. Nevertheless, since it was so important to impress her, I told her I was going to Cornell. Of course, I had never applied to Cornell and had only heard about the school through a friend. I also had heard it was somewhere in New York and hence maybe I could go. The last thing I wanted to say was that I was not going to college for she had been so kind to think of me as one of her friends and peers, all of whom were going to college. With that, however, I had to now figure out a way to get into college.

Luckily, there was an organization in New York City that helped kids like me go to college and before too long, although I never got to Cornell, I was accepted into the State University of New York, finished college, and went on to graduate school. However, the truth is that but for the young girl who posed the question about college I never would have gone. The lesson for me was that the aspirations that children have are so important to where they may end up in life. That the dreams we grow up with are often that which drive us, and often these visions need to be placed in the minds of children by those who care about them and their futures. Also, one's aspirations should never be limited by anything other than their imaginations. It seemed like such a simple act for her to ask me what college was I going to, yet her act did change my life. Life is made up of simple acts that later on are often found to be not so simple at all.

It was toward the end of my teen years as I was going off to college that I really began to get a better sense of the world. In fact, I remember leaving New York City and going to Long Island and, while doing so, discovering that most who lived there had backyards, tree-lined streets, the children went to schools with football and baseball fields, kids had grass to play on, and schools seemed neat and clean and even had tennis courts adjacent to their buildings. As I traveled farther I discovered that some homes were quite large, had three or four chimneys, so I knew those homes had at least as many fireplaces and probably a dozen or so bedrooms. There were open spaces in neighborhoods where people could walk or play golf and some homes even had swimming pools or ponds with ducks. All these things I had never seen before, and I never imagined people could have so much while others had so little.

In the neighborhood in which I grew up, trash was abundant, trees were rare, and rats would often enter your home and go through whatever food they might find in your kitchen. I began to witness these extremes, and it reminded me of that woman and her child I had seen when I was four and again brought home the fact that the world was simply not fair.

As I studied in college I also became more aware of the fact that money played a big role in the lives of all of us. That those who had it were advantaged in many ways and those who did not had far longer to travel as well as far more to overcome in order to get to the same place in life. Also, I came to believe that, although it might be somewhat acceptable for those with money to buy nicer clothes, bigger homes, a fancy car, a boat, or even to take a very nice family vacation, money or wealth shouldn't affect one's schooling, education, aspirations, or health. For those are the societal accoutrements that should be distributed equally to all regardless of wealth or status.

Throughout my college career and after I graduated, I did various kinds of community work that included travel and writing. I was, by this time, also affected by the civil rights movement in the United States and largely for that reason decided to become a lawyer. For some time I did civil rights work and criminal law, but eventually I returned to what I cared about most, and that was children.

It was after teaching for some years at the University of San Francisco School of Law and writing about children's law, as well as starting some local nonprofit organizations that worked to help inner-city kids, that I began to realize what I was doing was simply not enough, for even if I worked with all the children in the United States that would represent only about

4 percent of the children of the world. It was for this reason that I began to focus more and more on the world's children as well as on the women of the world who so often rear and nurture our children and, in doing so, play such a large role in crafting the world's future.

In deciding to embark upon international work, I worked first for the U.S. State Department and traveled to many countries and saw how people lived all over the world. I wrote reports on street children, prostitutes, and sex trafficking in Bangkok, Thailand. I visited children with AIDS in Botswana, as well as child soldiers in Rwanda, and explored the lives of those living in sewers in the underground world of Bucharest, Romania. In 1999, I received a phone call and was asked to write a report on the treatment of Tibetan children by the Chinese government. While writing this report, I was asked to travel to northern India and interview almost a hundred Tibetan children who had walked across the Himalayas in an effort to escape China and find some refuge at schools established by His Holiness the 14th Dalai Lama in northern India. It was during this period that I had the opportunity to meet with and befriend the Dalai Lama. We talked about the situation in Tibet, the lives of the refugees in India, the children who crossed the mountains, and the fact that he had not been to his homeland in forty years. We later also talked about something that has always troubled me, and that is how some people seem so narcissistic while others so selfless. How and why were some people so different and where does that come from? Are people simply born that way or are these attributes learned in one way or another? These are, of course, the kinds of questions that the Dalai Lama is often asked, and those who know him and who have had the opportunity to have these conversations have I am sure felt blessed.

At one such meeting with the Dalai Lama, when I asked him about compassion and the statement that is often attributed to him, "my religion is kindness," he told me that there are at least two levels of kindness or compassion. The first is the kindness that people should ordinarily show others regardless of their status in life, their differences of opinions, or historical events that may have somehow affected their feelings toward each other. His Holiness said that having an open heart toward others and showing them kindness is important to bringing peace to the world as well as to yourself. He also stated that there is a second and higher level of compassion, a level whereby people not only are kind to others but also act in some affirmative way to help relieve their suffering. He gave me the impression that it was not enough only to think kindly of others, but that people who are truly compassionate should do something to help.

With that thought in mind, in the fall of 2006 I decided to gather some of my friends and take them to India. I would introduce them to some of India's poor and forgotten people, and in doing so my friends, who I believed to be kind, would be moved to action, and in fact do something to help some of the world's poor. I called it a "donor trip," a trip whereby people who had far more than they needed were asked to consider giving of themselves and their resources to those who had very little. It was shortly after that donor trip that more and more friends began to give me money to help the extremely poor of India, and I decided to incorporate this effort of helping others less fortunate into a nonprofit organization specifically designed to help the poor and call it The Forgotten International.

The following are some of the beliefs that form the basis of this organization's work.

- That all people, regardless of where they happen to be born or live, are of equal human worth and deserving of the kindness of others.
- That in women and children, who are often the most defenseless among us, lie the hope and future of the world and, for that reason, they are most in need of the world's help.

- That in giving, the giver receives as much, if not more, than he or she gives.
- That we are all far more the same than we are different, and we should never let the differences that exist between us divide us.
- That goodness is the rule and evil the exception and, as such, we should trust in the basic goodness of all humankind.
- That ego, greed, and/or the lust for power are often responsible for much of the world's poverty and suffering. Hence these impulses should, at all cost, be resisted.
- That money is not the root of all evil but a means to an end, and that "end" can be to do good and relieve suffering. It is for us to choose.
- That the acquisition of wealth often has at least as much to do with luck and/or the service of others than it does a particular individual's skills, gifts, or ingenuity, and as such one's wealth should always be shared with those less fortunate.
- That nothing nurtures the world's people as much as the earth itself, and it is for that reason that the earth must be cared for in the same way that it cares for all of us. We are dependent on one another. It is a reciprocal relationship.
- That all of us have the opportunity to leave this earth better for having been here. It is what defines a meaningful life.
- That positive change often occurs through the work of many people making small contributions, and there is no problem too big as long as enough people care.

- That, on occasion, all of us who live comfortable lives should step out of what we know to experience the world outside of our privileged communities. No one should be allowed to simply ignore or forget the very many all over the world who have so little and suffer so much.

In an effort to further kindness through action, The Forgotten International works on four programmatic fronts. First, it provides mini grants to grassroots organizations around the world that work to alleviate poverty and the suffering often associated with poverty. Second, it sends skilled volunteers abroad to work with organizations that are trying to grow and help more and more people through the services they provide, primarily in the developing world. Third, on occasion it sends school supplies, clothing, shoes, toys, and medical equipment to people in need around the world. Fourth, it tries to provide some awareness about the poorest of the poor around the world and how easy it often is to help the so many who have so little. That is why this book was created and it is why we traveled to ten countries on four continents and here tell the stories behind the faces of the world's poor. Finally, and to all those who care, we ask that you consider helping one child, or one mother, or one family, or one school, or one village somewhere in the world out of poverty, and in doing so create a better future for those who will soon inherit the earth we share. Thank you so much.

Professor Thomas A. Nazario, President and Founder
The Forgotten International, www.theforgottenintl.org

When continuing to try to define who are the poor, others might simply say that one without a job or income is poor, or one who is homeless is poor, but that's not always the case either. Instead, it might be more accurate to assume that if one's "net worth" is zero or less, he or she is poor. One's net worth is that which is left after one subtracts that which one owes from the value of that which one possesses or one's assets. You might also be thought to be poor if the rest of your family is quite wealthy and you are not, or if your family is the poorest family in your neighborhood. Some have called this "relative poverty," those who are considered poor when compared to those around them. This may not find us the poor either, for if compared to a much larger group the relative poor may not be all that poor. The truth is that coming up with consensus as to who are the poor is not easy and sometimes is a matter of opinion. There is, however, a kind of poverty that exists in the world for which there is little dispute and that is the kind of poverty we will be exploring in this book.

This book is about the people around the world who live on less than a dollar a day and are considered among the poorest people on earth. The phrase "a dollar a day" was first coined by the World Bank in 1990 and has been used to connote an international poverty threshold that when used in some of the world's poorest countries to measure an individual's income provides the outside observer with some objective indication of the level of poverty in that region of the world. This, when compared to the cost of commodities in that area of the world, helps the observer assess one's level of poverty. In other words, this book is about the members of our human family who live at or below this poverty threshold and have either no income or very little income and yet often work hard but receive almost nothing for their labor.

Sometimes they are those who beg on streets, who live in slums or in makeshift homes with their children and other family members. They can be found in rural areas of the world where they may be subsistence farmers or farm the land of others or herd cattle and simply travel as nomads. More and more they are moving to big cities, often living on the street or living as squatters on lands that have been abandoned or are owned by the state. They may work in sweatshops, scavenge through garbage, or work at jobs that no one else would care to do. Often too they fish off boats they have lived on for generations, or go into mines to dig for ore that they bring to the surface for others, or decide to sell their bodies in the sex trade for this is the only thing they have of value and that they may use to survive and feed their children. They are extremely resourceful. They make do with what they have, but often suffer much in the process. The myriad of things the poor do to survive is certainly an aspect of their lives that we try to capture, but we also try to tell the stories behind the faces, of how so many around the world live day in and day out not knowing what the next day might bring.

They have been called the "extreme poor," or those living in "extreme poverty" (or absolute poverty, which is measured at a rate that falls below the "fixed" poverty threshold for the poorest countries in the world), and they live on the edge of life and death. If disease, war, or a natural disaster enters their world they simply die. In 2008, the World Bank revised the recognized international poverty threshold to $1.25 a day, and today that rate continues to reflect the average national poverty threshold among the poorest countries in the world.

Another very important thing to know about the people around the world who live in this kind of poverty is that most are *women and children*. This is so because women and children are most often those who are the least likely to be the principal breadwinners within a family unit, and because of their status have little access to any of the income that may be earned by a family. Also, women and children are often abandoned and left without support when men are lost to war or disease, take extremely dangerous or remote jobs, or simply leave them for another family. Women too are often forced to leave men as a result of the widespread violence perpetrated upon women by men

A group of homeless children sleeping on the streets of Bangkok, Thailand, many of whom are addicted to sniffing glue in order to suppress their appetite and in some ways psychologically escape their circumstances. They survive on the streets by nearly any means necessary but are more often victimized by others.

who have often fathered their children (domestic violence). This makes the world's women and children, along with the elderly, the infirm, and the disabled, the most vulnerable among us.

It would be very easy to come to the conclusion that if one only had limited resources and wished to help the poor of the world, women and children should be helped first. We believe this is true for at least three reasons. First, women and children are often the poorest of the poor, and so on moral grounds should be first in line for help. Second, women are often left to nurture and raise children, and so in helping women you help children, and in helping children you help women. Each is interdependent and connected, and both are indispensable to the future welfare of the world. Third, when helping women and children, such help may bring with it the gift of employment and/or education, and with that comes an opportunity to break the cycle of poverty. When women and girls receive economic help and acquire an income or an education, they become less dependent on men for their economic well-being, have fewer children, and work at jobs that bring them more self-esteem and self-confidence—all things necessary for a better life and for escaping poverty, if not for themselves then for their children.

One obvious question that comes to mind when one thinks about poverty is exactly *what are the effects or the results of poverty on one's life?* Often, the effects can be seen by simply visiting or spending time with some of the world's poor. Quickly, it becomes obvious what one lacks when one simply has little or no income. The truth is that the world today has become such that money buys everything, and without money, it becomes simply impossible to access even some of our most basic needs. Among them are food, clothing, education, health care, and shelter. Additionally poverty makes it very difficult, if not impossible, to access any legal rights. Often, too, those who are poor cannot afford to live in safe environments, are exposed to unsafe drinking water and toxic substances, and are often victimized as a result. Sometimes they are caught in conflicts over limited resources and have no ability to protect themselves. For many of

In Jessore, Bangladesh, the poor often make their homes in abandoned dwellings in order to reduce their expenses and gain some sort of protection for themselves, particularly in areas of the city that are not necessarily safe. This is a practice that holds true throughout the world.

who have "succeeded" in life, and possibly acquired some wealth, the wealth we acquired, although often a product of hard work, may have been a direct result of an education our family provided us or an inheritance given to us or simply a matter of being in the right place, at the right time, with the right idea. In other words, we benefit from the luck of the draw. The truth is that maybe for many of us who are comfortable, that comfort may be owed to our parents, to our friends, or to the society at large that have made opportunities available to us and not to others. We have been blessed. We have been lucky and not all we possess has been the direct result of our own ingenuities and talent. It's important to recognize that. Therefore, the notion of sharing, or "giving back," is not a prerogative but instead an obligation to return some of the good fortune we have had to whence it came, the world at large. Third, it can be argued that sharing one's wealth and good fortune with those less fortunate is in our self-interest, for the more that others are content in their own lives the less resentment they may harbor. In fact, history has proven that where great disparities in society exist, and millions upon millions struggle with nothing, then conditions are ripe for revolution, violence, and crime. Therefore, the more secure and content you make your neighbors, the happier and safer we all will be. Finally, and as an extra bonus, one rarely gets more pleasure than when helping others.

A Word About the Rich

Believe it or not, years ago there were simply no rich people on earth. In fact, but for a few exceptions related to royalty, conquests, and dynasties, all of us had about the same amount of wealth and, in short, that was very little. We were all poor. Great and vast differences in wealth, and the accumulation of wealth, began to become common only some two hundred years ago with the advent of imperialism, the industrial revolution, the discovery of great deposits of natural resources, the age of great inventions, the growth of capitalism, world trade, the advent of technology, and other new sources of great wealth. Also, with

such great wealth having been created, one's definition of who are the rich has changed, and although some sixty years ago millionaires were somewhat rare and thought to be rich, today they are a dime a dozen. Moreover, as the numbers of rich have increased, the amount of wealth they possess has multiplied exponentially. This has created a new class of world billionaires and has enormously increased the size of the chasm that exists between the world's rich and the world's poor. For some, this chasm has grown so large and so deep that it has become morally unacceptable and very difficult to justify.

As of the publication of this book, *Forbes* magazine has put the number of people throughout the world who personally possess more than $1 billion at 1,426. By the way, one billion is equal to one thousand million. Of these 1,426 individuals, 442 are from the United States (about 31 percent). That is quite high; nevertheless, it's a percentage that has been sinking in recent years with more and more billionaires coming from large developing countries such as China and India. Today, China, if one includes Hong Kong, has 161 billionaires and India has 55, two countries that also have hundreds of millions of the world's poor. Moreover, these 1,426 individuals possess an average of $3.8 billion each, which has gone up by $100 million over a one-year period, from 2012 to 2013. Hence, together, these billionaires are worth roughly $5.4 trillion and, as many have said, while many of the world's poor get poorer, the rich get richer.

In order to give some perspective as to what all this means, believe it or not:

- Many of the richest people in the world make more money in one minute than nearly a third of the world's poorest people make in a year.
- In 2012, each of the world's 1,426 billionaires made an average of $273,973 a day. That is more money than that made by 20 of the world's poor over the course of their lifetimes.

Marjyama, 27, the mother of 2-year-old twin girls, has been living for two years under a "Do Not Urinate" sign in the city of Accra, Ghana, in West Africa. She came to the city seeking work but now hopes to someday return to her home in a farming village in the north and once again be near family.

- The ten richest people on earth together have a net worth of $451.5 billion. That is 61 percent more money than the country of India spends annually to care for the needs of one sixth of the world's people.
- The combined wealth of the 100 richest people in the world is $1.9 trillion. That is more money than is possessed by the governments that have to serve the needs of more than half of the world's people.

What is also hard to believe is that, in spite of the vastness in the disparities of wealth that exist in the world, the extent to which the rich have been allowed to get richer has gone unregulated. This is because many societies believe, particularly since the advent of capitalism, that if people are allowed to build large companies and enter into great endeavors and are later rewarded with large profits and high salaries this benefits society at large, and at the same time it encourages others to follow in their path of entrepreneurship and economic expansion.

On the other hand, today many believe that allowing for such disparities in wealth is not necessary in order to encourage hard work, ingenuity, and the entrepreneurial spirit and that no person needs this kind of wealth in order to be motivated or to provide a very comfortable life for themselves and their families. In an effort to further this belief, some governments around the world have made efforts, and are continuing to make efforts, to do more and more to slow the growth of these disparities by creating laws that impose higher taxes on the wealthy, taxes on large inheritances, and tax laws that encourage or reward those who give away much of their wealth to charity and the needy. Countries that are just beginning to create large numbers of people with great wealth are still, however, considering how best to share that wealth among their people and provide for the welfare of their poor. There is still much to be done in this area of social policy, wealth transfer, and economic justice. ∎

Rudra, 5, and his sister Suhani, 3, search for tea to drink at the Charan slum settlement in Dharamsala, India, where they live with their family. They survive although two of their siblings recently died of malnutrition.

A Way to Help

If you would like to help alleviate poverty and the suffering often associated with poverty, consider contacting one or more of the organizations below and ask how you can get involved.

ACTIONAID

ActionAid is an international antipoverty agency that works to end poverty and injustice in forty-nine countries worldwide. In doing so, it works with local partners and together helps secure the rights to food, shelter, work, education, health care, and a voice in the decisions that affect the lives of millions of the world's poor.

Address: ActionAid
1420 K St., NW, Suite 900
Washington, DC 20005
Phone: (202) 835-1240
Email: info@actionaid.org
Website: www.actionaidusa.org

AMERICAN JEWISH WORLD SERVICE

American Jewish World Service is an international organization, with hundreds of grassroots organizations in the developing world, with an emphasis on promoting good health, economic development, disaster relief, and political and social change. Its members work with women, youth, ethnic, religious, and sexual minorities, indigenous displaced people, refugees, and people living with HIV/AIDS.

Address: American Jewish World Service
131 Steuart St., Suite #200
San Francisco, CA 94105
Phone: (415) 593-3280
Email: ajws@ajws.org
Website: www.ajws.org

CATHOLIC RELIEF SERVICES

Catholic Relief Services carries out the commitment of the Bishops of the United States to assist the poor and vulnerable overseas. It works to promote human development by responding to major emergencies, fighting disease and poverty, and nurturing peaceful and just societies worldwide. As part of the universal mission of the Catholic Church, its members work with local, national, and international Catholic institutions and structures, as well as other organizations, to assist people on the basis of need, not creed, race, or nationality.

Address: Catholic Relief Services
228 W. Lexington St.
Baltimore, MD 21201
Phone: (877) 435-7277
Email: info@crs.org, crswest@crs.org
Website: www.crs.org

CARE INTERNTIONAL

CARE International is dedicated to ending poverty worldwide, advocating for global responsibility through strengthening the capacity for self-help, providing economic opportunity, delivering relief in emergencies, influencing policy decisions at all levels, and addressing discrimination in all its forms.

Address: CARE International
465 California St., Suite #1210
San Francisco, CA 94104
Phone: (415) 781-1585
Website: www.care.org

HEIFER INTERNATIONAL

Heifer International works with families and communities around the world to end world hunger and poverty by empowering individuals to create income streams so that they can better feed their families and become self-reliant. Heifer provides gifts of livestock and training to help families improve their lives in sustainable ways. In exchange for the livestock and training, families agree to give one of the animal's offspring to another family in need.

Address: Heifer International
1 World Ave.
Little Rock, AR 72202
Phone: (855) 948-6437
Email: info@heifer.org
Website: www.heifer.org

GLOBAL EXCHANGE

Global Exchange is an education and action resource center, which for the past twenty years has been working internationally on issues ranging from human rights to economic justice, centering its efforts to help transform the global economy from a profit-centered society to a more communal-centered world.

Address: Global Exchange
2017 Mission St., 2nd Floor
San Francisco, CA 94110
Phone: (415) 255-7296
Email: web@globalexchange.org
Website: www.globalexchange.org

OXFAM INTERNATIONAL

Oxfam is an international relief and development organization that creates lasting solutions to poverty, hunger, and injustice. Oxfam is an international confederation of seventeen organizations networked together in ninety-two countries where they are saving lives and helping people overcome poverty while fighting for social injustice.

Address: Oxfam America
             226 Causeway St., 5th Floor
             Boston, MA 02114
Phone: (800) 776-9326
Email: info@oxfamamerica.org
Website: www.oxfamamerica.org

PEACE CORPS

Peace Corps volunteers help countless individuals who want to build a better life for themselves, their children, and their communities by providing trained men and women in all parts of a community.

Address: Peace Corps
             1111 20th St., NW
             Washington, DC 20526
Phone: (855) 855-1961
Email: Form online
Website: www.peacecorps.gov

ROTARY INTERNATIONAL

Rotary International has 33,000 Rotary clubs in more than two hundred countries, helping to promote peace through the improvement of health, the support of education, and the alleviation of poverty. Through its more than 1.2 million members, Rotarians provide humanitarian services and help build goodwill and peace throughout the world, which is supported by voluntary contributions from Rotarians around the globe.

Address: One Rotary Center
             1560 Sherman Ave.
             Evanston, IL 60201
Phone: (866) 976-8279
Email: Contact.center@rotary.org
Website: www.rotary.org

UNESCO

UNESCO's mission is to contribute to the building of peace, the eradication of poverty, sustainable development, and intercultural dialogue through education, the sciences, culture, communication, and information. It does much of its work in Africa and is particularly concerned with issues related to gender equality.

Address: UNESCO
             7 Place Fontenoy, 75352
             Paris, 07 SP, France
Phone: +33 (0)1 45 68 1000
Email: Form online
Website: www.unesco.org

UN VOLUNTEERS

United Nations Volunteers recruits global volunteers for peace and development and in doing so partners with governments and nonprofit and private sector organizations in order to support development programs.

Address: United Nations Volunteers
             Postfach 260 111
             D-53153 Bonn, Germany
Phone: +49 228 815 2000
Email: information@unvolunteers.org
Website: www.unv.org

WORLD FOOD PROGRAMME

The World Food Programme is the world's largest humanitarian agency fighting hunger worldwide. In doing so it works to help reduce chronic hunger and to save, restore, rebuild, and protect the livelihoods of the world's poor.

Address: World Food Programme
             Via C.G. Viola 68
             Parco dei Medici
             00148 Rome, Italy
Phone: +39 06 65131
Email: form online
Website: www.wfp.org

CHAPTER TWO

Subsistence Living and the World's Rural Poor

No book about the world's poor would be of any worth without some discussion about the way most of the poor manage to support and care for themselves each day. "Subsistence living" is the term that today is being used more and more to describe the lives of those around the world who, often due to their impoverished condition, make use of what they have access to, as well as their surroundings, to provide themselves and their families with the basic necessities of life. This includes those who survive by farming the land as well as fishing the sea and the waterways of the world. Today, this kind of living or lifestyle supports nearly 2.5 billion people on earth and, by far and away, represents the main means by which most of the world's poor get through their lives each day. The largest percentage of those who live in this manner are subsistence farmers.

In an effort to further define these terms, one should know that subsistence farmers, at least in the strict sense, are people who work small plots of land all over the world with the primary intent of producing enough food each year to feed themselves and their families. In other words, they owe their subsistence, and in a real sense their survival, to the land and what it produces or fails to produce for them. Those who are strict subsistence farmers are often so not because they wish

In the town of Mae Sot, Thailand, Burmese refugees often take seasonal jobs that require them to spray insecticides over large tracts of land. They do so with little protective gear, but it is what they feel they must do in order to support their families.

to be, but because either they have so little land that all they can hope to produce, even under ideal circumstances, would be enough food to feed their families or the land they have is so depleted of minerals that they would be lucky to produce enough food to feed their families. This is the unfortunate circumstance of millions upon millions of people around the world.

Some subsistence farmers can, with some consistency, produce more than what they might need to care for the immediate nutritional needs of their families. They might be called the lucky ones, and each year they begin their work with the hope that not only will they produce enough to feed themselves and their families but that they will also be able to get some part of their harvest to market. Of course, when their harvest is sold (or bartered for other goods), they use that income to provide their families with some of the additional necessities of life, including shelter, fuel, other types of food, possibly some medical care, and even some schooling for their children. In any event, the lives of subsistence farmers are far from easy, and for most who work at subsistence farming the truth is that, throughout much of any given year, there is seldom enough food to eat. In fact, 50 percent of all subsistence farmers and their families worldwide are undernourished, and in Africa three-quarters of the continent's malnourished children can be found on small farms. Together the world's subsistence farmers make up about 75 percent of our planet's rural poor. This is largely true whether or not they try to simply feed themselves or are occasionally able to get some of their harvest to market.

Additionally, many of the men, women, and children around the world who either directly or indirectly live off the land are not farmers in the traditional sense, but instead may be herders of livestock, sometimes their own, and sometimes owned by others. Some too are nomads who travel the rural and marginal areas of the world often characterized by harsh conditions and scarce resources that are spread out over pastoral lands, deserts, or tundra. Nomads and seminomadic communities come in three types.

In the back roads of Ghana, the women and girls of Nkwanta are often seen carrying overhead large buckets of cassava (a starchy edible root), which they farm and then bring home to their villages. It serves as a staple in their diet.

A TYPICAL SUBSISTENCE FARMER

• She is a woman, typically between 20 and 35 years of age.

• She often works on less than two hectares of land.

• She earns less than a dollar a day.

• She has few resources, such as money, credit, fertilizer, technology, or sometimes even water.

• She often cannot meet her family's daily needs for food, shelter, or health care.

• She is completely vulnerable.

There are those who live with their livestock on pastoral lands. They can be found in the highlands of the Himalayas and Mongolia. There are the hunter-gatherers of the Amazon rain forests, the hill tribe areas of Southeast Asia, the Canadian Arctic, and much of Africa, and there are the traders of crafts, day workers, and musicians, namely the Roma who, although originally from India, now can be found throughout Europe.

Many nomads and seminomadic communities have tribal associations and today their continued livelihood is at risk due to the increasing governmental takeover and the privatization of what was once open lands. The rest of those around the world who live off the land, about 1.5 billion of them, live as subsistence farmers and work on one of some 470 million small plots of land in mostly India, China, Southeast Asia, Africa, and Latin America. Together, they produce slightly over 50 percent of the world's agricultural crop. In Latin America, for example, some 17 million farmers work over a third of the total cultivated land to produce more than half of the maize and three-quarters of the beans consumed domestically. In Asia, some 200 million farmers cultivate small plots of rice. In India, more than 70 percent of the milk is produced by households with only one or two milk-producing animals.

Also many of the subsistence farmers throughout the world do not own the land they work; instead they either appropriate rural lands for their own use (in many parts of the world this is not necessarily illegal) or are working the land of another. Moreover, when they are not working their own land, they may be working under the direction of someone who may be managing many plots of land for a wealthy individual or company. Nevertheless, these subsistence farmers are in reality sharecroppers who in return for farming these lands are allowed to live on the land and keep sometimes up to 50 percent of the proceeds from the sale of what they harvest and sell. For this income, these farmers usually have to work the land all day, pay for and plant seeds, purchase fertilizer (when needed and available), and sell the crop. If the landowner contributes to the cost of irrigation, provides the seed, fertilizer, and insecticides, often the farmer's pay is reduced to one third of the crop yield. Again, this is very little and often keeps many of these landless farmers in extreme poverty. This practice is very common throughout India as well as other parts of the world.

Of course, the biggest problem associated with life as a subsistence farmer is that these people are food insecure and are left very vulnerable. In short, they are forced to live a life on the edge. This is true not only as to the farmers themselves but also as to their children who often work the land as well. Hence, if there is a conflict in the area and security is interrupted, if there is a flood, a drought, the loss of a family member who works the land, a disagreement with the landowner or the government about the use of the land, a drop in the value of one's crops or increase in the cost of fertilizers, all could be lost. Since, too, that which they harvest often represents the only source of income and survival for a family of subsistence farmers, when a change of this nature occurs either the family starves to death, the family must move on in the hope of finding other work or food, or the family ends up displaced among beggars or in a refugee camp awaiting international aid, which may not come soon enough.

Text continues on page 52

Like Maria Lucia Quisepe, 80, sitting right, the women of El Alto, Bolivia, who survive as subsistence farmers during the week, come to market each Sunday to sell their fruits and vegetables in hopes of making a little extra income.

Nora Huanca Illari, 11, tosses potatoes to her mother, Manuela Illari, 45, as they farm land in a field outside of Santiago de Okola, Bolivia. They work for some potatoes and food for their animals. Nora goes to school every morning and in the afternoon she works with her family in the fields until sunset. In the background is the mountain known as the Sleeping Dragon.

Farming in Bolivia's Countryside

THE ILLARI FAMILY

In the fields outside of Santiago de Okola, Bolivia, families often work together to harvest potatoes to feed their families. The Huanca Illari family works every day until dusk on land owned by Manuela Quispe Avile. At approximately 11,000 feet, not only is the sun quite intense but days and nights can get very cold. Manuela Illari (45) is the mother of two girls who help her in the fields daily. Berta, who is only one year old, does what she can but is often cared for by her sister, Nora, who is 11 years of age. Manuela Quispe Avile is 70 years of age and owns the property they work. She works along with the others to help bring in the harvest.

In return for their work the Illari family is given some of what they have harvested, enough to feed themselves and other members of their family. Also, and on occasion, when the harvest goes well, they can sell some of what they receive to others or trade the food for other goods or services.

Toward day's end, the children's grandmother sometimes takes a moment to dance with Manuela as a kind of celebratory gesture. No music is ever necessary.

Left: Dominga Illari, 70, left, and Manuela Quispe Avile, 70, right, dance after harvesting potatoes at the end of the day as the rest of the family looks on in the photo above.

JACABA COAQUISA ILLARI

In a nearby field, 80-year-old Jacaba Coaquisa Illari, a widow, works in her field from 7:30 A.M. until dusk gathering oats and green beans. This year the crops from her land were affected by a lack of rain and an early frost that stopped her crops from growing. As a result many of her green beans were small and brown, good only for making flour but not for eating. The oats in her field were also affected by weather and turned yellow too soon. Her crops are her subsistence. She sells nothing at market and what she grows must last her all year. When she gets sick or hungry she borrows a phone from a neighbor and calls one of her children. They live in the city of

La Paz, some distance away. Luckily she has seven children, who visit on occasion. They likely keep her alive.

Later in the day, Jacaba cuts grass for her animals. Recently she had to sell her cow and donkey because she could not afford to feed them. She walked five hours to the closest town to sell them. Today all she has left are five sheep.

Likely few people on earth have worked as hard or as long as Jacaba has throughout her life. The condition of her hands tells that story. ∎

Above: The hard-worked hands of Jacaba Coaquisa, 80, holding the green beans she grew on her land.

Right: Jacaba walks through her oat field, which turned yellow too early due to an unexpected change in the weather that has largely ruined her harvest.

The Roma of Eastern Europe

The Roma people are in fact widely dispersed throughout the world. However, they are most often associated with living in and around central and eastern Europe. The Roma also sometimes go by different names depending on which area of the world they may happen to be living in, but in short they are an ethnic group who are known to be seminomadic. Often, the Roma people temporarily settle down in various areas of cities or rural locales that have been either abandoned or seemingly little used by others. The Roma are known in the English-speaking world by the term "Gypsies." It is today, however, thought to be a somewhat derogatory term and to be avoided.

The estimated number of Roma living throughout the world varies considerably. The reason for this is that many of them travel from country to country and often have no papers, no identification, and no birth certificates that indicate where they were born. Also, and for a variety of reasons, many Roma choose not to register their ethnic identity, and so census figures have always been difficult to acquire. Estimates range from 5 to 14 million Roma worldwide, with their heaviest concentrations in Europe.

The Roma have been discriminated against in a variety of ways throughout their history. They have nevertheless continued to survive, although often living in extreme poverty. Throughout the streets of many cities in Europe you will find Roma children begging or selling wares that their parents may have made. Most Roma survive through craft making, such as that of wooden spoons and dolls. Some are miners, some are gold- or silversmiths, many are musicians, florists, and in parts of Romania, animal trainers, such as bears, for local carnivals.

VIRGIL LENTEA AND STELA PAUN

The Roma of eastern Europe live in very harsh conditions and have lived in this part of the world for decades. Virgil Lentea and Stela Paun are both 60 years of age. Virgil is Stela's second husband. Her first husband died some years ago after they had had five children, four boys and a girl. All the children left them as the family traveled through Europe. She believes that the children now live somewhere in Germany, though she has not heard from them in some time. Virgil, too, has four daughters. He also does not hear from his children very often and for this reason has written their names on his hand so as not to forget them.

Virgil Lentea, 60, and his wife, Stela Paun, 60, are members of the Roma community. Here they take a moment to talk about the loss of their horse, which used to pull their cart. In the background is the house they live in, but do not own, in Slatina, Romania.

Virgil used to make wooden spoons and sell them to shop owners who would in turn sell them to tourists throughout Europe. The spoons never brought him much money and he is now too old to work. He has no income, no papers, and no identification of any kind.

Stela has diabetes but gets free medicine from a local clinic. She also gets 120 lei ($38 U.S.) a month from the government. This money and three chickens is all they have to survive on each month. When asked what they use for food, they say they eat eggs and snails that they happen to find around their home. The house they live in does not belong to them and can be taken away by the mayor of the village at any time. They used to have a horse but it died. Now they are left with just the cart that the horse used to pull.

Their day's activities revolve around trying to keep warm, collecting wood for a fire, and finding whatever food they need to survive. They have no electricity, no soap, no toothpaste, no hot water, and of course, most of the time, no money. When asked what they most wish for, they said they wish they had more medicine, more light, some occasional warm food, and maybe another horse. They expect little to change throughout what remains of their lives.

THE GULIE FAMILY

In the country of Romania, where Virgil and Stela have their home, lives another Roma family called the Gulies. The Gulie family of five live in a one-room home and struggle each day to survive. The mother, Viorica (31), got married when she was 16 years of age and shortly thereafter had a daughter, Marinela.

Marinela is now 12. Her dad, who is often away, works but makes little more than 10 lei ($3.15) a day. The home is shared by Viorica, daughter Marinela, a son named Dubu (11), and her youngest child, Alex (6), as well as Viorica's mother-in-law, Constanta (58). All of them get up at 6 A.M. and start their day by trying to warm the house, then feed their two pigs, and then get Alex off to school. He goes to school from 8 to 12 P.M., only half days, while his older siblings go to school from 12 to 5 P.M.

Viorica spends most of her day collecting garbage for their pigs, as well as plastic bottles that she can sell to recyclers. On occasion, she might find fresh fruit within the garbage. Often they eat that

Far left: Viorica Gulie, 31, and her three children stand in the doorway of their home in Slatina, Romania. Above: Later in the day she searches for scraps in the garbage to feed her family's pigs.

Living on the Catch

Each day they dock their boat along the Tonle Sap and Mekong River banks of Phnom Penh, Cambodia. They are the You family. They have seven children, the oldest is 24, the youngest is 4. They have lived along the river banks of this area of the world for over thirty years, since the fall of the Khmer Rouge in 1979. They own no land, have no home on shore, and all they have in the world in the way of material possessions is their fishing boat. They said, "Other than our one boat and a few chickens living with us, we have nothing."

Their life consists of fishing every day, often going out for miles to better their chance at catching enough fish to feed the family and, on occasion, others. On any given day, the family patriarch, Mr. You, spends as much time mending well-worn fishing nets as he does fishing. He does not have another job; all he knows is fishing. When there are no fish, he often has to borrow money from local lenders at high interest rates since he has no credit or collateral, at least the kind of credit or collateral that any commercial bank would respect. It is the only way he can provide for his family.

On long days while waiting to catch a fish or two, Mr. You worries about his children and the life that may be in store for them. His older children sometimes go fishing with him, but the younger ones wait for him

Docked on the shores of the Mekong and Tonle Sap Rivers, in Phnom Penh, Cambodia, these families live their whole lives and carry on all of their daily activities on small boats. At dusk, You Hai Yati, 4, washes herself in these waters. It is the same water that she and her family drink and use to cook every day.

The children of these fishing families often assist their parents to bring in the daily catch, but as a result they often do not attend school and grow up to carry on the same lifestyle as their parents for generations to come. This child (right) at age 4 has already started down this path.

by the shore. He worries about them and their safety. None of his children have ever gone to school, nor will they. There is simply no money to pay the school fees at state-run schools, and he often needs his children around to help him. Fishing is their only job and their only means of subsistence.

The You family, and generations before them, have been fishing these waterways for decades, but more recently their lives have become harder. Fewer and fewer fish has caused malnutrition while polluted waters have created illnesses related to the ingestion of toxic substances. Moreover, when a family member gets sick, there is often no money for a doctor. Also, with the growth of cities, markets, and tourism, fishing families are often not welcomed at places where they have docked their boat for years. As a result, they are often forced to move and find another place where they can stay, even if temporarily.

When asked about what hopes they may have for their children and the future, they responded, "We hope that our children will follow in our footsteps, for we have offered them nothing that would help them improve their lives." Hence, they said, "We live without hope for a better future." When asked if their exists any kind of safety net, government help, community organizations, or family help, they said, "Nothing, only when we go out to fish, our older children must look after the young." When asked if they are happy, the You family said, "When fishing is good, we can make enough money to pay back our debts and purchase needed supplies, but when fishing is not good, often we can make only a few dollars a day and that's only when we have caught enough fish to sell at the market. Most of the year, we simply live hand to mouth and try to keep our stomachs full." This is the life of fishing families in this part of the world. ∎

In the evening fishing families spend time repairing their nets by the lights of the city in order to make sure they are prepared to fish the next day.

Sometimes, too, a family that lives on the edge, as these families do, do not have to experience an international disaster to lose everything. For example, a family may simply lose a goat or a cow, a cow whose milk fed their children and whose surplus milk was sold to neighbors for additional income or whose dung was burned for fuel to heat their dwelling or to cook their food. Also, and in an emergency, it is sometimes a cow or a goat that can be bartered or sold to save the family's land, purchase needed essentials, or save a child's life who is very much in need of medical care. With the loss of something as seemingly inconsequential as a farm animal, an entire family's circumstances can spiral downward and easily end very tragically. Indeed, subsistence farming is a precarious way to get through life, for "subsistence" is just that, nothing more.

Finally, and as noted above, in addition to those who live off the land, there are those who live off the sea and the waterways that may surround their village or local communities. Many of these families have fished to live for years, if not generations. Others do so as new immigrants or refugees who fish and live on small boats lined up along beaches, rivers, or inland bays because it may be the easiest way to acquire food and provide for some sort of shelter for one's family. These fishing families work at fishing with the same intentions as subsistence farmers: to feed their immediate family and relatives and, if possible, sell surplus fish at market in order to provide themselves with some income. About 40 million people around the world fish in order to provide for themselves and their families, and in doing so feed about 200 million people daily. Subsistence fishing is most common throughout Southeast Asia, the Mekong River basin, Indonesia, the Amazon region, and parts of Africa.

Problems, of course, exist here as well, which relate to the overfishing of waterways and the reduction of catch for sale. Also more and more of the fish that people around the world consume is being taken out of polluted water. This pollution threatens human health as well as the health and numbers of many species of fish around the world. All of this increases the time, the risk, and the cost associated with catching enough healthy fish to meet the needs of families who depend on fishing as their principal food source and usually their only income stream.

A Word About the Simple Life

When reflecting on the lives of those around the world who live possessing only the bare minimum of modern conveniences and often work the land or live off the sea, it is important not to confuse their plight with those who may wish to lead a simple life free from many of the "conveniences" of the modern world. The truth is that many around the world who are relatively poor and live with very little are not necessarily poor in the sense of deprivation. In fact, they may have all they need to lead relatively happy and healthy lives. Their fisheries may be clean and not overfished, and their land, what little they have of it, may have been kind to them over the years. They, too, may love their simple life. Remember, what we see through the lens of the developed world may be laced with distorted assumptions about what one needs to lead a happy and healthy life, so we should always try to avoid making hasty assumptions about another's way of life. To illustrate this point, take for example the famous story of one Greek fisherman.

By a boat docked in a tiny Greek village an American tourist passes by and compliments a Greek fisherman on the quality of his fish and asked how long it took him to catch them.

"Not very long," answered the fisherman.
"But then, why didn't you stay out longer and catch more?" asked the American.
The Greek explained that his small catch was sufficient to meet his needs and those of his family.
The American asked, "But what do you do with the rest of your time?"

As seen on page 26, here the same seasonal worker is spraying insecticide over fields in Mae Sot, Thailand, to provide for his family of six, despite the fact that he has malaria.

CHAPTER THREE

Slums: The Home of So Many

Outside Phnom Penh, Cambodia, Panha Sak, 2, runs alongside the polluted waterways of his home. This area also doubles as his playground.

We have all seen the places around the world where the poor live, and in fact regardless of where one lives one does not have to travel far to find the poor. They can be found in the richest countries in the world as well as, of course, the poorest. The poor can also be found in rural areas of the countryside, off the side of a road, in a small village, behind an industrial area of a medium-size city, near a polluted waterway, a city dump, or in some vacant lot not too far from a local shopping area or market. In some cases, the poor can be found right outside our doors or just down the block. Knowing this, some people often seek to avoid the poor by purposely maneuvering around certain neighborhoods or parts of a city or even countries where one might think too many poor people live. Sometimes we do this because we don't want to be reminded about the poverty that exists around us, or we wish to avoid the poor because of fears we have about our own safety. Sometimes it may be because we feel guilty about what we have while so many others have so little. Certainly, it is always difficult to see and acknowledge the poverty and suffering that many experience around the world. Nevertheless, for whatever reason, it's not unusual to speak with fairly well-to-do people in a given country and discover that they know little about the lives of the poor and

The sun goes down in the urban sprawl of El Alto, one of the poorest cities in Latin America, located just outside of Bolivia's capital of La Paz. It is home to some one million people who live in more than their fair share of slums as well as an oppressively high altitude. Also unique to this city is that, due to climate change, glaciers have dried up and snow packs are disappearing, leaving this city with very little water. It is a city in distress.

the number of poor people who live near and around them.

Putting all of the above aside, however, I would guess if we posed the question "Where do the world's poor live?" to a random group of people, most would either name a particular country or continent or simply say that there are slums all over the world. Certainly the world's slums would be a good answer, for many millions of the world's poor do live in slums, and although, as suggested above, the poor can be found everywhere and anywhere, slums are places where great concentrations of the world's poor live. The numbers of people who actually live in the slums of the world, however, change with one's definition of a slum. So what is a slum?

Technically, slums are not defined by the people who live there but by the condition of the housing and services that exist there. In short, slums are defined by characteristics that relate to the quality of housing and surrounding conditions of a particular residential area, characteristics that are often far below the housing standards offered to people with greater resources in that particular part of the world. Typically slums are places where one would find housing that has been built in violation of housing or health codes (if any even exist), where there may be limited electricity or clean water, few toilets, little in the way of health-related services, sometimes few or poor schools, and often lacking in sanitation and garbage collection or disposal. It is hard to say how many people in the world live in these kinds of conditions; however, in 2010 the Population Institute stated that 32.7 percent of those who live in the cities of the developing world live in slums and estimated that, worldwide, somewhere between 800 million and a billion people live in slums of one kind or another, a figure that will likely double by 2030.

Of course slums, which are usually found in large cities, often provide the only means of shelter for some of the poor of a particular locale. Often, too, one will find high rates of illiteracy, unemployment, and overcrowding in many of the slums of the world. Today, probably the most famous slum in the world gained its notoriety from the movie *Slumdog Millionaire*. The slum that was captured in that movie is called Dharavi, in Mumbai, India. It is one of the world's largest slums with an estimated population of a million people. Nevertheless, if one visits that slum, one would see that it is largely a city within a city. People who live there generate their own economy, whereby they purchase, sell, and trade with one another. Many have found sources of electricity, some have a television and refrigeration, and although the dwellings are small, most live quite harmoniously on their limited incomes with their neighbors who are trying to survive in many of the same ways as they do.

This is not to say that there isn't resentment or even anger and hatred toward slum settlements as well as the poor of India and elsewhere. Many believe that the poor are parasites and add little to the economy or the overall well-being of society. In general, it is believed the poor are lazy, often commit crimes, and are more trouble than they are worth. The truth is that the poor often work harder and longer for their meager incomes than many other individuals who work for substantially more money. In fact, those who live in the slums of our cities often do the work no one else would care to do, such as street sweeping, recycling, and the house work of millions, and in doing so they provide a very cheap labor force. There is also little evidence that the poor are more inclined to commit crimes than any other segment of our global community. Nevertheless, these strongly held beliefs remain common among many and often shape the policies created by governments that affect the poor worldwide.

Another of the world's most famous slums, called Kibera, is located on the outskirts of Nairobi, Kenya. It is the second largest slum in Africa with an estimated 5,000 structures and a population of about 250,000 inhabitants. Conditions in this slum are extremely poor with almost no access to electricity or running water. The Kibera settlement is nearly a hundred years old and was settled when Nubian soldiers were awarded plots of land in

this location when they returned from their service in the First World War. Over time, the British colonial government allowed the settlement to grow as tribes moved into the area to rent land from Nubian landlords. Although this slum has seen many changes over the years and is one of the most studied slums in the world, it remains in need of much help from the outside world and is heavily polluted by garbage, soot, and other wastes, including human and animal feces from open toilets. These conditions, coupled with poor nutrition, account for much of the illness and disease found there.

There are many other slums all over the world, particularly in developing countries, which although they may not be as large as Dharavi or as studied as Kibera are in some ways even more difficult places to live. Many of these slums are in South and Central America, Mexico and Africa and are often found on the outskirts of cities. These slums almost always have no electricity, few roads, no bathrooms or toilets, and of course little or no heat, clean water, or sanitation to speak of. How the poor live around the world varies to some extent. Some have nearly nothing and may live in a forgotten area of the countryside, and others have at least enough to survive with some dignity as long as life does not deal them an unfortunate blow.

Text continues on page 68

In Bucharest, Romania, some of the city's poor climb down into underground heating vents or sewers (left), where they live and eat by candlelight for there is no electricity. Right: Here Hora Florin, 28, a victim of the Romanian dictator Nicolae Ceaşescu's orphanages and one of Romania's lost generation of children, lives underground where the heating vents keep him warm at night.

on many different factors. It is during the winter months (November through April) when she and her family often struggle most, for it is then that much of whatever she can earn doing odd jobs goes toward the cost of gas, wood, charcoal, and electricity to keep the house warm. Winters are harsh and long in Moldova and without some heat in this part of the world people die. Lidia's ability to earn income is also affected by the fact that her 4-year-old daughter Anastasia requires care during the day and such care at a nursery school or elsewhere is far more than Lidia can afford. Hence, Lidia must watch over her throughout her working day.

Lidia's husband died eight years ago. She is her family's sole source of income. When things get really bad, she borrows what she can and begs and prays for the rest. On a typical day Lidia is up by 6 A.M. and lights a fire for heat and cooking. She may make a little breakfast for the kids, then feeds the animals (which include chickens, geese, dogs, and their cat). In the spring and fall, Lidia goes off with her daughter to work in the agricultural fields of Moldova. There she plants and helps with the harvest. She is paid with either food or cash, whatever she can negotiate.

Ion, her son, goes off to school in the morning and when he returns home does his chores, including chopping wood, carrying water to the house, and feeding the animals. When his mother returns home they eat together, he takes a bath, and then he does his homework.

Ion's younger sister Anastasia was born with some type of speech impediment. Although approaching five years of age she doesn't speak. Nevertheless, she is clearly smart and understands

everything. Everyone who knows her says she is the sweetest child in the world.

Lidia has lived this way since her husband died. The house she lives in is not hers but instead belongs to a "boyfriend," who is Anastasia's father and works as a mechanic in the city of Chișinău (the capital of Moldova). He comes by the house every three months or so but never brings home any money. Other than their clothing, Lidia and her children own nothing.

Asked whether she believes life for her will ever get better, she said, "Maybe not now, not the next year, but the children will grow up and they will have a better life — and if that is not to be then maybe their children will have a better life." ■

Far left: Anastasia, 4, hugs her favorite pet as her brother attends to his chores around the house. Above: Lidia Potcovi-rova can't afford to send Anastasia to school so her daughter often accompanies her mother to work in the fields. They live in Fintinita, Moldova.

The Singh Family

There are seven members of the Singh family. They live in a slum called Kusum Pahari in New Delhi, India. The slum itself is one of as many as a thousand such pocket slums that exist in New Delhi. Approximately 1,200 people live here. Sona Devi (35) is the mother of five children ranging in age from 2 to 12 years old, and she works from dawn to dusk taking care of her children and seeing to it that they get at least one meal a day and that they don't get lost among the mazelike passageways of this somewhat hectic and fast-moving area of the city.

The slum itself is located, in part, on top of a garbage heap between several hotels and is relatively close to an affluent area of the city. For that reason, the slum has been scheduled for demolition. The city of New Delhi wishes to use the property, and so it must be cleared for development. The Singh family has lived here for twenty-five years. This is also true for many of the residents of this slum, and although they have been told they must move, they have no place to go. Several organizations have come to the defense of these slum residents and are asking the city to postpone the demolition until better plans have been made for their relocation. The lack of this kind of planning,

of course, is not at all unusual. Hopefully, the Singh family, along with many of the longtime residents of the Kusum Pahari slum, will be relocated to an area that provides them with continued access to family, friends, employment, schools, and other civic amenities that they and their children will need in the future.

Sona Devi, after washing clothes, feeding the children, and cleaning up the small area that she and her family occupy in the world, sometimes goes off to clean the homes of wealthy residents nearby. This helps her husband support the family as she has been able to earn about 300 rupees (about $7 U.S.) per month. Her husband, Kamal Singh, who is 50 years old, works throughout the city sweeping streets in the morning before residents leave to go to work or to the market. On a good month, he might also find work doing construction at someone's residence or possibly some street repair work around the city. If he is lucky, over the course of a month he can make as much as 3,000 rupees (about $70). That, along with his wife's income, is all the money Mr. and Mrs. Singh make to support their five children.

The Singh family lives in a 8 x 9–foot room in a makeshift house. The house itself is made of adobe/

Sona Devi, 35, washing clothes as five of her children look on from the small one-room brick structure they all live in with her husband, Kamal Singh.

Left: Three of Sona Devi's boys play on the only bed they have for the entire family. From the left are Ajit Kumar, 5, Dilip Kumar, 9, and Kuldeep Kumar, 10. Above: Shambati, 42, a neighbor of Sona Devi, cooks dinner outdoors over an open fire for her husband and three children.

clay-like material and their one-room home provides them with their living and sleeping quarters. The cooking of meals takes place outdoors in a wood-burning fire container. None of the dwellings in this slum have bathrooms or running water. The families who live in Kusum Pahari urinate and defecate outdoors, usually on top of the garbage heaps or behind some bushes or near an animal watering hole. This is not unusual, and in fact about a third of the world's people don't have toilets and simply relieve themselves in riverbeds, woods, or some discreet area or wherever possible. Women, of course, have more trouble taking care of their needs in this manner because they have greater privacy

Power throughout the slum is obtained illegally but few seem to care. Different households splice into a single power source and as a result electrical wires travel throughout the slum. It is not the safest way to get power to homes but it does make a big difference in their lives.

The children of the Singh family work as well. For example, the family's 6-year-old son, Vishal, often wanders through the garbage heaps collecting rags and putting them in a bag for recycling. The rags are scattered throughout the area's garbage heaps. These rags are later sorted, washed, and made into various kinds of cottonwares in factories throughout India. Vishal often pushes aside dogs and pigs as he sorts through the garbage to find the rags. The pigs that live throughout this slum feed on the garbage. They are owned by slum dwellers who butcher them and sell their meat at the markets throughout the slum. Chickens also wander through the garbage, picking at whatever they can find to eat. The chickens are owned by slum dwellers who, when the need arises, pluck, clean, and cook them to feed their families or sell at the market. For Vishal's labor, he earns about 2 rupees (less than 5 cents) a day.

Vishal also spends time taking care of other children, and although he is only 6, he often takes care of his 2-year-old sister while his mother attends to other chores. Children here don't get paid for taking care of other children, it's simply part of their contribution to the family and community. Some say that children taking care of other children makes them more responsible when they become adults. Nevertheless, for children all around the world, the

Above: Vishal Singh, 6, searches for rags to recycle among the garbage dump behind his home while a young child in the background defecates in the same area.
Far right: Children bounce a ball as they play among pigs and garbage in this slum.

concerns and are sometimes at risk whenever they go off alone to relieve themselves. In many parts of India, as well as the rest of the world, women try not to drink too much water in order to avoid having to urinate. They do this as a means of self-protection as the lack of a safe private space leaves them very vulnerable. Of course, this is just one of the by-products of being poor. Drinking water, too, must be brought in by truck to this slum every few days. The water is carried in plastic containers by residents and is used sparingly because deliveries are often late and summers in New Delhi often reach 120 degrees Fahrenheit.

responsibility of caring for other children occupies many of their growing-up years.

When Vishal is not working or attending to his chores, he attends a school for the children of the Kusum Pahari slum. It is located on the slum grounds. The school is an open-air facility. It has no power, no toilets, and no books. To learn their lessons the children and teachers here work off chalkboards. Tuition is 2 rupees a week but no child is turned away for lack of funds. When Vishal is not working, he goes off to school with nearly six hundred other children of this slum community. With a little luck and a little schooling, life may hold some better opportunities for Vishal in the future. ■

Left: In the Kusum Pahari slum in New Delhi, as is true in slums throughout India, residents splice into electrical outposts in order to bring power to their makeshift homes.

Right: Also true among the poor is the fact that children everywhere take care of other children. Here Vishal Singh, 6, cares for a baby girl while her mother is away.

Phay Chakrya, 32, who is HIV positive, sits by the doorway of her home in a slum outside of Phnom Penh, Cambodia, and wonders what is next in life for her. She and her family are squatters who do not own the home they live in and are likely to be evicted soon, but of course they have no place to go.

Squatters: When One Has No Place to Live

THE SRAH CHAK COMMUNE

Phay Chakrya (32) sits by the doorway of a wood shack constructed decades ago near Boeng Kak Lake in the Srah Chak commune in the Daun Penh District of Phnom Penh, Cambodia. The shack has, since 1991, served as her home, and the area itself is home to many of Phnom Penh's extreme poor.

She lives here with her father, Phay Phanna (60), who lost his leg when he stepped on a land mine in 1988 near the Cambodian-Thai border. In 2009, Mr. Phanna also lost his wife, Nhem Sophann, to cancer and now is the sole head of the family left to try and care for eleven children in a home he does not own and is scheduled for demolition since being purchased by a private developer in 2008. In this slum live many other families. Hundreds have already been evicted. Mr. Phanna says that none of the families have been compensated in any way for all they have lost. Some now live on the streets of Phnom Penh and others have moved to the countryside hoping to find work or shelter. Mr. Phanna awaits to hear his fate and that of his family for then he will have to decide what to do and where to go.

Phay Chakrya awaits, too, anxious to hear her fate and that of her family. While she waits she has much to ponder. She also has faced great loss. She has been HIV positive since 1999, a disease she contracted from her husband, who has since left her. They had two children together. Both have now died of AIDS. They simply had no access to the medical treatment that might possibly have saved their children or at least prolonged their lives. Her despair is written on her face.

Some members of the family find odd jobs in Phnom Penh to help support the family, but Mr. Phanna still spends most of his days remembering his wife and what things used to be like when she was alive. It is what takes up his time at least until they are eventually evicted.

**Left: Mr. Phanna, the family's patriarch, seeks an afternoon breeze by the doorway of his makeshift home, which overlooks the polluted waterway that surrounds them daily.
Top right: Mr. Phanna struggles to move about their small home with crutches. He knows too that it will be difficult for him to travel when they are evicted.**

ON THE STREET IN BUCHAREST

This is the home of a family that has decided to wrap some plastic tarp around some heating pipes in a park located in a rather wealthy area of Bucharest, Romania. The heating pipes provide them with at least a little heat, which keeps them alive throughout the cold winters in this part of the world. The makeshift home is occupied by a man who works in and around the neighborhood helping to carry groceries home for the wealthy residents. Living with him is his pregnant wife, their two children, and his sister. They have lived like this for two years, and when there is not

Above: In Bucharest, Romania, the Opiteanu family built their home around heating pipes that can be found throughout the city.
Right: Their 15-month-old, Robert Opiteanu, peers out of a clear panel of the tent home his family lives in. It is all they have.

Left: Alina Opiteanu repackages flowers she bought to resell outside her home in order to try and make some extra money to feed her family.

Above: Alina along with her husband, their children, and her sister-in-law all share this very limited space.

enough money coming into the household they supplement their income by selling flowers at the market. Their tarp home is an improvement from the days when they simply lived on the street. The adults escaped from abusive families or orphanages when they were teenagers. The community has let them live under their tarp in spite of the fact that they are squatting on public land. In fact, sometimes people leave them food to eat. Nevertheless, as another winter approaches, it's a wonder nothing else can be done for them. At some point they will have to move.

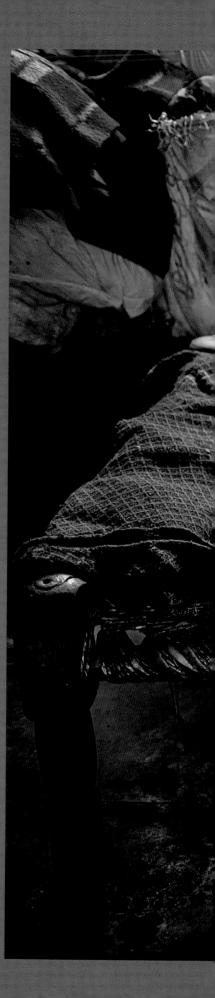

LIVING NEAR A RIVER EAST OF DELHI

By the side of the Yamuna River in Sarai Kale Kahn, New Delhi, India, Sunita Devi (24) fans her infant son Hemant in III-degree heat inside a concrete structure she lives in with two families. These families live temporarily on what is government property. They will stay there until they are kicked out because they have no other place to go. At the top of the photo, cow dung is stacked. This family uses the dung as fuel for cooking their food and warming their shelter. Sunita's husband, Kailesh Chand (26), who sits with his son Om Prakash (2), is a machine operator. It is a job his brother had before he lost his leg in a work-related accident.

Above: Sunita Devi, 24, fans her infant son near a pile of cow dung in an effort to protect him from flies and the heat of central India.

Right: Kailesh Chand, 26, sits with his son Om Prakash, 2, at the same squatter encampment.

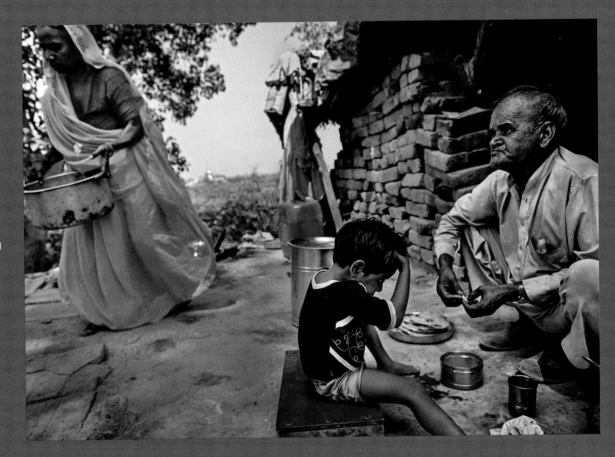

Left: Siblings Rohit Kumar, 4, left, and Khushi Devi, 6, right, take a break from playing and stand outside the building they and their parents occupy in Sarai Kale Khan in New Delhi. Right: At the same squatter encampment, Rampiari Devi, wearing a bright pink sari, works to prepare food for her family.

Rampiari Devi, a neighbor who lives next to Kailesh Chand, works carrying water from the nearby river to help prepare the day's meal. When asked about her age, she said she believed she was somewhere between 55 and 60 years of age. Many around the world don't know exactly how old they are. Often, she and her husband, Harpal Singh (60), make some extra money by carrying bricks in and around local construction sites or sweeping city streets. When they do so, they can make as much as 68 rupees or about $1.30 a day. With that they can buy a package of lentils or a kilo of rice or flour. It is food they and their granddaughter Dalawati Devi (4) need to survive. On occasion, the brickyard allows Rampiari and Harpal to take some bricks home. They use them to add a little additional space to their living quarters.

Rohit Kumar (4) and his sister Khushi Devi (6) also live in this abandoned structure. Their parents work as gardeners in a nursery and together earn 100 to 150 rupees ($1.90–$2.85) a day. These families, which together have almost forty people associated with them, share three rooms in this structure. Electricity is quite irregular and, on a good day, they may get two hours of power. They get the water they need from the river. Easy access to the water is why they stay, and it is why so many of the world's hundreds of millions of squatters live in and around waterways. ■

few legal rights to the property they've settled. Hence, for them, their lives and rights are far more precarious, and what rights if any they have depends on a variety of circumstances, most of which may be outside their control.

A Word About the Rights of Squatters to Shelter

As mentioned earlier, squatters can be distinguished from more traditional slum residents in that squatters generally have few, if any, property rights. They have simply appropriated lands, constructed makeshift housing, and decided to live at particular locales because they provide them with access to some kind of work or subsistence as well as services they may need for themselves and their families. Sometimes they have lived in these locales for decades. The dwellings they have built, although often made out of materials that others have thrown away, may be quite substantial and provide them and their families with the only home and shelter they have. Nevertheless, and because they often have no legal right to the property they are on, their options are very often not as broad or significant as more traditional slum residents.

In short, the rights of squatters throughout the world vary greatly and depend on a variety of circumstances, most important, the country in which they live and whether that country has been inclined to be respectful of the poor. This is true in spite of the fact that international laws and instruments exist that seek to encourage and protect the rights of the poor to adequate housing. Nevertheless, international bodies recognize that many impoverished countries can do only so much to help their poor and that in spite of international law the world is still largely run by sovereign nations and it is the law of those countries that is most often relied upon to help their residents. Some countries have conditioned the rights of squatters on factors that relate to how long they have been occupying a particular piece of property, how long the squatter community itself has actually been in existence, how many people and families are occupying the prop-

erty, whether the occupants have given the property owner some notice of their existence, whether the squatters have a working relationship with the government, and whether the property that is being occupied is private or public in nature. Also important to know is whether the land being occupied is part of a public right-of-way that needs to be cleared to construct a road or provide access to others and whether the land has a school on its grounds or a place of worship.

In some countries, where millions of people have lived as squatters for years, the laws can be quite elaborate and respectful of squatters' rights. For example, in India, that nation's High Court in 2009 held that the poor, regardless of whether they are squatters or slum residents with traditional property rights, should be given assistance in relocation to other areas of a city when they need to be moved for purposes of development. In doing so, the court stressed that measures should be taken so as not to leave those relocated in a worse position than before they were forced to move. One cannot simply demolish a person's dwelling place without advance notice and some plan to help them start new lives. In fact, the High Court of India recognized that even squatters have a fundamental right to a livelihood and shelter as well as access to civic amenities, public transportation, and a life with some dignity.

In other and more developed countries, such as those in northern Europe and in the United States, squatters are sometimes entitled to due process rights and must be given their day in court before they can be evicted from a particular piece of property. The law does not allow property owners to take the law into their own hands and simply evict people by force, even if they are there illegally. In the overwhelming majority of countries, however, the reality is that squatters have almost no rights except possibly for being given some notice that they must gather their belongings and leave before their dwellings are demolished. It is a constant worry that affects millions of slum dwellers and squatters worldwide. ■

Sam Kim Heng, 47 (front), sits in front of the residence of Cambodia's prime minister and protests with others who have been displaced and have no homes. They are rubber plantation workers who have been evicted from land owned by a local businessman. They are hoping the prime minister will find them someplace to live.

A Way to Help

If you would like to help alleviate poverty and the suffering often associated with poverty, consider contacting one or more of the organizations below and ask how you can get involved.

ACTIONAID SOUTH AFRICA

ActionAid provides local partners with the help they need to fight poverty and injustice worldwide. In doing so, the right to food, shelter, work, education, health care, and a voice in the decisions that affect the lives of the poorest of the poor has historically been its principal concern.

Address: 108 Fox St.
            Metropolitan Building, 8th Flr.
            Johannesburg, 2000 South Africa
Phone: +27 11 731 4566
Email: sheila.cochrane@actionaid.org
Website: www.actionaid.org/southafrica

DEVELOPMENT ALTERNATIVES GROUP

Development Alternatives Group provides the means for creating sustainable livelihoods on a large scale to impoverished communities throughout India. It does so through the use of appropriate technologies, effective institutional systems, and environmental and resource management methods in its efforts to mobilize widespread action to eradicate poverty and regenerate the environment.

Address: B-32, Tara Crescent
            Qutub Institutional Area
            New Delhi - 110016 India
Phone: 91 (11) 2656-4444, 2654-4100
Email: tara@devalt.org
Website: www.devalt.org

DUSHTHA SHASTHYA KENDRA (DSK)

Dushtha Shasthya Kendra provides various social and economic programs to the economically depressed and vulnerable groups throughout Bangladesh. Women are of particular concern to DSK, and so are specifically targeted by its programs. Empowerment of communities is a central focus of all of DSK's development initiatives, and over the years the organization has extended its geographical, beneficiary, and programmatic coverage quite significantly. Programs include work, education, health, microfinance, agriculture, water supply, and sanitation.

Address: House-741, Road-9, Baitul Aman
            Housing Society
            Dhaka – 1207, Bangladesh
Phone: 880-2-9128520
Email: info@dskbangladesh.org
Website: www.dskbangladesh.org

HOMELESS PEOPLE'S FEDERATION PHILIPPINES

Homeless People's Federation Philippines helps poor community organizations in cities across the Philippines find solutions to problems they face with securing land, housing, income, infrastructure, health, welfare, and access to affordable credit.

Address: 221 Tandang Sora Avenue
            Quezon City, Philippines
Phone: (632) 455-9480
Email: pacsil@info.com.ph
Website: www.hpfpi-pacsii.org

HUMAN RIGHTS LAW NETWORK

Human Rights Law Network provides free legal services, conducts public interest litigation, engages in advocacy, conducts legal awareness programs, investigates violations, publishes "know your rights" materials, and participates in campaigns throughout India to help the poor. HRLN works with other human rights groups and grassroots organizations to enforce the rights of poor marginalized people and to challenge oppression, exploitation, and discrimination against any group or individual on the grounds of caste, gender, disability, age, religion, language, ethnic group, sexual orientation, and health, economic, or social status.

Address: 576, Masjid Road, Jungpura
            New Delhi - 110014 India
Phone: +91-11-24374501
Email: contact@hrin.org
Website: www.hrln.org/hrln

MANGO TREE GOA

Mango Tree Goa provides help to slum and street children in India. From its base in Goa, it provides food, shelter, medical care, and education for some of the poorest children in India. In a safe, playful environment, children receive a fun and creative education and also have plenty of time to do what children the world over should do, which is PLAY!

Address: "The Mango House"
            House No. 148/3
            Near Vrundavan Hospital
            Karaswada, Mapusa, Bardez
            Goa - 403526, India
Phone: 0091 9881 261 886
Email: info@mangotreegoa.org
Website: www.mangotreegoa.org

PINGALWARA SOCIETY

Pingalwara Society provides a home for the underprivileged and mentally challenged. It serves as a school, medical center, orphanage, and all-around center for help for those who are disabled, neglected, injured, or simply have no place to go.

Address: G T Road, Amritsar - 143 001
             Punjab, India
Phone: +91-183-584713, 584586
Email: pingal@jla.vsnl.net.in
Website: www.pingalwaraonline.net

SHACK/SLUM DWELLERS INTERNATIONAL

Shack/Slum Dwellers International provides the poor urban communities from cities across South Africa and around the world with problem solving strategies adapted to the myriad of problems often faced by slum dwellers. Since SDI is focused on the local needs of slum dwellers, it has developed the experience needed to advance the common agenda of creating "pro-poor" cities that integrate, rather than marginalize, the interests of slum dwellers in their respective approaches to urban development.

Address: 1st Floor
             Cnr Raapenberg and Surrey Rds.
             Mowbray, Cape Town 7700
             South Africa
Phone: (+27) 21 689 9408
Email: sdi@courc.co.za
Website: www.sdinet.org

SLUMS INFORMATION DEVELOPMENT AND RESOURCE CENTER (SIDAREC)

Slums Information Development and Resource Center provides youth development projects in the slums of Nairobi. The organization was established in 1997 as a community-based youth group with an aim of tapping and consolidating skills and talents existing among the youth in the community for the common benefit of slum dwellers.

Address: P.O. Box 9687-00300
             Nairobi, Kenya
Phone: 254-020-2246961
Email: info@sidarec.org
Website: www.sidarec.org

THE SOCIETY FOR THE PROMOTION OF AREA RESOURCE CENTRES (SPARC) IN ALLIANCE WITH MAHILA MILAN AND NATIONAL SLUM DWELLERS FEDERATION (NSDF)

SPARC provides the administrative support necessary for an alliance of agencies working with slum dwellers to be successful. This alliance organizes and mobilizes the urban poor and negotiates with resource-providing institutions. NSDF works in twenty-one of India's cities with local groups such as the Railway Slum Dwellers' Federation and the Airports Slum Dwellers' Federation, which are made up of families living alongside the railway tracks and on land owned by the national Airports Authority in Mumbai. Mahila Milan is also part of the alliance and supports and trains women's collectives to administer and manage their community's resources and participates in NSDF activities.

Address: 2nd Floor, Khetwadi Municipal
             School Building
             Khetwadi Lane, No. 1
             Girgaum, Mumbai 400004
             India
Phone: +91 22 23865053/23858785
Email: sparcnsdfmm@gmail.com
Website: www.sparcindia.org
             www.nirman.org

UN-HABITAT

The United Nations agency for human settlements is UN-HABITAT. It is mandated by the UN General Assembly to promote social and environmentally sustainable towns and cities with the goal of providing adequate shelter for all.

Address: P.O. Box 30030, GPO
             Nairobi, 00100, Kenya
Phone: (254-20) 7621234
Email: infohabitat@unhabitat.org
Website: www.unhabitat.org

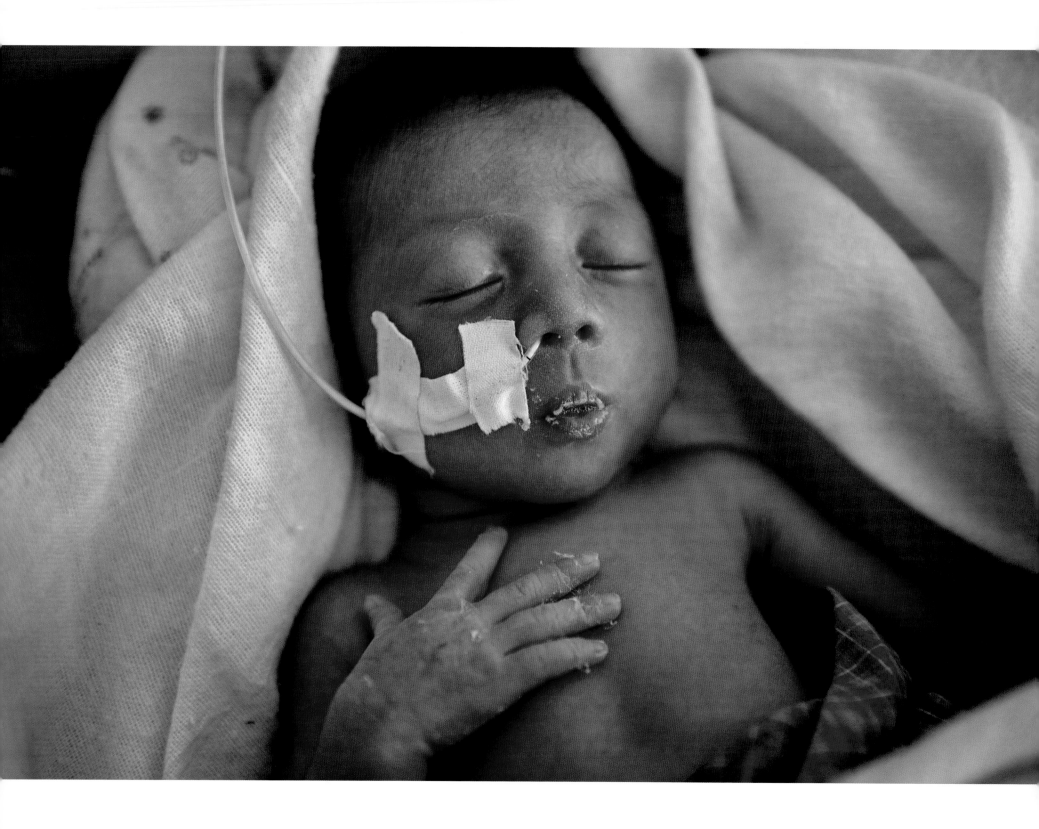

CHAPTER FOUR

Health Care and the Poor

For those who work with the poor around the world, one thing that quickly becomes quite obvious is the relationship between poverty, health, and health care. This is true in any country, even rich countries where those who are poor often experience less than adequate health care services, while those who have at least some wealth can use it to access better health care, not only for themselves but also for their families. This disparity in services was noted nearly fifty years ago when, in 1966, Dr. Martin Luther King, Jr. stated:

"Of all the forms of inequity, injustice in health care is the most shocking and inhumane."

Interestingly enough, long ago there was little distinction between the health care provided to those with means and the health care provided to the poor. For the truth was that some two hundred years ago there were few medical advances, fancy hospitals, well-trained doctors, long-term care facilities, or drugs that would help improve one's quality of life or prolong their lives. Also, and as noted in chapter 1, in the past there were few great disparities in wealth and much of the world was equally poor.

A baby girl, 25 days old, hangs on to life in the premature birth unit of Mae Tao Clinic in Mae Sot, Thailand. Her 22-year-old mother works as a farm laborer who had to return to work and could not stay at a hospital. The infant weighs 3.5 pounds. She will likely live.

Today, of course, things are quite different. Good or excellent health care has become available in many parts of the world. There have been great advances in medicine, new diagnostic techniques, and much has been learned about the transmission of diseases as well as disease prevention. Unfortunately, however, to a large extent, good or excellent health care has become a commodity that can be purchased in much the same way as one would purchase food, livestock, a house, a car, or a good education for one's child. So although many believe that all people should have equal access to the same health care services regardless of wealth, this is simply not the case. Those who are poor, again regardless of where they might live, simply cannot access the same kind or quality of health care as can those who are more privileged. It is this "injustice in health care" that Dr. Martin Luther King, Jr. spoke about years ago and found so shocking and inhumane.

What are some of the barriers that exist to health care?
With regard to health and health care, the problems of the poor center around two issues. The first is the issue of access. One barrier here is that the cost of health care services and medications are often far more than what the poor can afford. This is particularly true in countries where health care insurance does not exist, governmental health care programs are very limited, or health care programs and services are simply beyond the reach of what a particular country may be able to provide. Also, in many countries, health care services are physically out of the reach of the poor. The closest doctor may be many miles away. Hospitals and clinics are few and far between. Institutions of higher learning in these countries may also be ill-equipped to train doctors or other medical professionals. As a result, in many parts of the world, medical service providers are far outnumbered by those in need of their services, and medical care, particularly in the case of an emergency, may simply be practically impossible to obtain.

In recent years the lack of available doctors and other

TEN COUNTRIES WITH THE SHORTEST LIFE EXPECTANCIES		TEN COUNTRIES WITH THE LONGEST LIFE EXPECTANCIES	
I. Swaziland	39.6 years	I. Japan	82.6 years
2. Mozambique	42.1 years	2. Hong Kong	82.2 years
3. Zambia	42.4 years	3. Iceland	81.8 years
4. Sierra Leone	42.6 years	4. Switzerland	81.7 years
5. Lesotho	42.6 years	5. Australia	81.2 years
6. Zimbabwe	43.5 years	6. Spain	80.9 years
7. Afghanistan	43.8 years	7. Sweden	80.9 years
8. Central African Rep.	44.7 years	8. Israel	80.7 years
9. Liberia	45.7 years	9. Macao	80.7 years
10. Rwanda	46.2 years	10. France	80.7 years

medical professionals has been made worse by the fact that the shortage of needed medical professionalals has also been felt throughout the developed world. As a result many doctors and nurses, who may have received their training in poor and less advanced countries, are now being recruited by rich countries to work in the developed world, and in as much as these practitioners can make more money abroad they often leave their home countries. This only adds to the continued shortage of medical professionals in the areas of the world where they are needed most. For example, Africa and Southeast Asia together share, and attempt to address, 58 percent of the world's health needs, but to do so they have only 15 percent of the world's health care providers. On the other hand, Europe and the Americas together service about 20 percent of the world's health needs but employ 65 percent of the world's health care workforce to do so. Additionally, and as a further illustration of this problem, at any given time one will find just five or fewer physicians for every 100,000 people in any of the fifteen countries that make up sub-Saharan Africa. In the United States the ratio is one doctor for every 390 residents. It is no wonder so many of the world's poor and underserved people die. In fact, it has been said that one of the biggest killers in the world is the distance between the poor and a doctor.

The second major problem associated with health care and the poor relates to the quality of care. People who live in large cities, or in the Western or developed world, can ordinarily, at least if they have some means, access a relatively modern facility and receive adequate or better medical care. Some of the best doctors and hospitals in the world can be found in the United States, northern Europe, and Australia. Major cities in Asia also attract fine doctors, and resources exist in those cities to build impressive health care delivery systems. However, citizens of the rest of the world, particularly those who live outside of major cities and who may not have the financial resources to access quality care, must settle for what is left. In those circumstances, care might be provided at a local clinic, a mobile medical unit, by a nurse or nurse practitioner, midwife, pharmacist, herbalist, or traditional or spiritual healer. Few of the facilities available to the poor around the world, however, have advanced medical equipment, the latest drugs, highly trained doctors, or even the basic equipment needed to help diagnose a particular ailment. And it is because of both the lack of access to medical care as well as the diminished quality of care that is provided to the poor that great problems continue to exist in health care for the world's people. This is what continues to leave nearly a billion people without any meaningful access to health care each year.

What happens when one lacks access to health care?

Of course, one of the results of the lack of health care is its effect on the length of a person's life. More people today are dying young. For example, in the countries where health care is scarce, the average life span of the population is rarely much longer than forty to fifty years. Conversely, in countries where advanced medical care has been made available to all and treatment includes prevention and education about one's diet as well as the environ-

THE DISEASES THAT TAKE THE LIVES OF THE CHILDREN OF THE POOR

In many of the poorest countries of the world, where 17–20 percent of all children die before their fifth birthday, it is often the lack of health care that takes them. These children die as a result of immunizations they never received, food that is not available, or water that is simply not suitable for drinking. The resulting diseases themselves vary, but nearly all could have been prevented if medical care, food, and clean water were readily available. Of all such diseases, pneumonia takes the most children, but diarrheal diseases as well as parasitic diseases come in a close second. These diseases are most often contracted through the ingestion of polluted water. Moreover, of those children who survive these illnesses, many are left crippled or disabled for life.

On the other hand, less than 1 percent of children in more developed countries die before their fifth birthday. What this means is that of the 1,000 children born in countries such as Afghanistan, Angola, Chad, the Democratic Republic of the Congo, Guinea-Bissau, Mali, Sierra Leone, and Somalia, about 174 will die before they reach 5 years of age. However, in countries such as Finland, Greece, Iceland, Japan, Liechtenstein, the Netherlands, Spain, Sweden, and Switzerland, only about 3 children out of that same random grouping of 1,000 children will die before their fifth birthday. This is simply more evidence of the disparities that exist in world health and the injustice with respect to who lives and dies.

Disease	Deaths Annually
Pneumonia	1,600,000
Diarrheal disease	1,100,000
Infections	1,000,000
Malaria	950,000
Asphyxia	800,000

Note: Measles and AIDS together take another 700,000 children each year while malnutrition is implicated in up to 50 percent of all these child deaths.

WHY IS THERE A WORLD FOOD SHORTAGE?

With so much food in the world, or at least an ability to produce it, why do so many go hungry? It's been called "food security" and it is achieved when all people, at all times, have physical and economic access to sufficient, safe, and nutritious food to meet their daily dietary needs and food preferences for an active and healthy life. Some reasons why food security has yet to be achieved for so many are as follows.

- **The failure of distribution.** The truth is that it is very difficult to distribute nonperishable food all over the world and have it in place when needed. However, more and more world food organizations are now considering locales around the world that would store food specifically to deal with the world's needs.

- **Food tariffs, quotas, and/or subsidies.** In some cases fees are placed on foods coming into a country or subsidies are paid to farmers to produce or not produce food. These policies affect the price of food worldwide and sometimes can create food shortages as well as spikes in the price of food. This makes it difficult for the poor to access the food they need.

- **Crop failure.** Crop failures occur as a result of drought, flood, deforestation, or the fact that the land intended to produce the food has been stripped of the minerals necessary to produce a healthy crop. When crop failures occur, food shortages follow, and people go hungry.

- **The damming of riverways.** Closely related to a crop failure is the situation whereby a country may dam a river and in the process destroy the fisheries of those downstream. The "crop" here are fish. A crop for which hundreds of millions of people depend on for their survival (see chapter I). Also, the damming of riverways or the loss of mountain glaciers because of global warming reduces the amount of water available for communities downstream. Less water, fewer crops, less food.

- **Growing population and growing demand.** With the growth in population, particularly in China and India, there are more and more people on earth to feed. Also, as more people move to cities and generate higher wages for themselves, they create a greater demand for more expensive and processed foods. These demands create shortages or price fluctuations within the food supply, which often affect the poor most and again can create food shortages.

- **Rising fuel costs.** With rising fuel costs around the world it has become more and more expensive to transport food. This affects the market price of food and again makes it more difficult for the poor to purchase the food they need.

- **Conversion of crops to biofuel.** Some countries are now attempting to use crops that would otherwise be produced to feed the world to create biofuels for automobiles. This reduces the production of certain crops thereby inflating the cost of related foods and creating price hikes.

- **Conflicts.** Major conflicts of almost any kind disrupt food production or the transport of food to needed areas of the world. Also, internal conflicts may displace people from their lands and push them into areas where food shortages exist.

Note: A Right to Food. Today, more and more people are suggesting that there exists a right to food. In fact, at least three international treaties arguably provide for such a right, and about a quarter of the world's countries either explicitly or implicitly attempt to establish this right for their citizens through their constitutions. Today, approximately a dozen countries around the world actually provide for entitlement programs to help maintain the food security of its citizens through specific national legislation or court rulings. As of yet, however, effectuating this right remains largely uneven at best, and in a majority of nations around the world ready access to food is far from a reality, and the understanding of this "right," its content, limitation, and application by oversight mechanisms, remains largely ill-defined.

Amakumah, 26, lives in the village of Kabiti in the country of Ghana. Here, she stirs peppers over an indoor open fire to make soup for her family. This is, however, the kind of indoor cooking practiced in many parts of the world that is so damaging to the health of the world's poor.

mental hazards that can lead to a variety of illnesses, average life spans are sometimes over 80 years.

Some of the other realities of life that can, of course, affect one's health as well as his or her life expectancy are: war or conflicts within a country of one kind or another; violence, domestic or otherwise; the presence of famine; the lack of immunizations; and the presence of environmental toxins, such as water and air pollution, whether outside or inside one's living quarters. For example, in many areas of the world, heat is produced and food is cooked in open containers or fire pits that burn wood,

cattle dung, or other solid fuels within the home. Nearly half of the world's people depend on such fuels as their main energy source, and this is very common in households in slums or in some colder rural areas. Unfortunately, there is often very little or poor ventilation within these living quarters, and consequently the smoke produced is inhaled by the residents. This smoke is often quite toxic. It damages lungs and creates long-term respiratory problems. It has been estimated that 1.6 million people die each year as a direct result of smoke inhaled in their homes while heating or cooking food for their families, 500,000 in India alone, most are women. Moreover, 3.8 million poor women are burned by these fires each year and are often disfigured for life or die as a result. Poor children, too, are lost in the same manner, and although efforts have been under way to create safer stoves for the millions of the world's poor, so far these new stoves have not reached the people who need them most.

What about world hunger and the poor?

With regard to world hunger, health, and the poor, it can be easily said that with poverty comes hunger, and with hunger comes the need for health care. The role that hunger plays in the world is significant. In fact, of the 7 billion people on earth, somewhere between 925 million and 1.1 billion people are considered undernourished and go hungry for at least some substantial time over the course of any given year. Of this figure, 780 million suffer from "chronic hunger." Most chronic hunger occurs in Asia, in particular Southeast Asia, Africa, as well as Latin America and the Caribbean. Overall, 95 percent of it occurs in the developing world. Such hunger leaves children severely malnourished and stunts their growth for life. In many cases it also affects brain growth, IQ, and the ability to learn and progress at a normal rate. It has also been estimated that 10 percent to 15 percent of all health ailments experienced worldwide are, in one way or another, related to malnutrition, and of course malnutrition is directly related to poverty.

Tragically, it is the children of the poor who suffer most. As noted above, many millions of children around the world suffer from malnutrition. In many cases, however, these children do survive. Nevertheless, in an unacceptable number of cases there are children who do not. It has been estimated that of the 7 million children under the age of 5 who die each year, nearly 60 percent of these deaths are caused by malnutrition or hunger-related diseases. When children die of hunger, it often occurs early in life. Sometimes these children are born to a mother who is simply so malnourished herself that she cannot produce the

breast milk necessary to feed her child, and over the course of several weeks the infant dies. In other cases, where children live longer, it is their overall weakness that takes them. They either cannot survive an illness, fail to get enough calories to acquire the weight and strength they need to keep their heart and muscles moving, or simply pass overnight, a result that is not unusual in some parts of the world. Sometimes, too, mothers who have several children and no means to support or feed them select a child, often the weakest, that they know will not survive, and purposely decide not to feed that child so that others in the family might have enough food to live. This is probably the worst case scenario, but nevertheless it is what some do who have lost access to food for an extended period of time and have to make very difficult choices for the sake of all of their children.

In spite of all the hunger that exists in the world, many believe that each year the world does or can produce enough food to feed the world's people and more. Few experts dispute

Text continues on page 112

Above: In the Charan slum settlement of northern India, this mother starves one of her children in order to better elicit the sympathy of others and raise more money through begging to feed the remainder of her family. Right: This child at age 2 weighs only 9 pounds.

The Mae Tao Clinic: Help for the Poor

The Mae Tao Clinic in Mae Sot, Thailand, was established in 1989 by Dr. Cynthia Maung. It exists on donations. The clinic is free and provides emergency care for the poorest of the poor in this part of the world. Its patients are often Thai farmworkers or Burmese refugees, some of whom cross the Moei River, which lies between Burma and Thailand, at great risk to themselves and their families.

The baby lying in the arms of her father has no name. She is five months old and suffers from severe burns when she spilled a pot of hot water over herself while she was being watched by her 11-year-old sibling. Her father, Zaw Win, has spent the last three days at the clinic with her. He is a farmer and is losing pay while he tends to his child. He said they are at this clinic because he and his family had "no other place to go." Another one of this baby's siblings looks on while their father hopes for the best.

Soe Min is a 24-year-old farmer from a township in Burma. Although he is yet to be diagnosed, the staff at the clinic believe he is suffering from appendicitis or a bowel obstruction, which is quite painful and has caused him to vomit almost continuously for the past two days. In an effort to comfort him, his sister Pan Phyu rubs her brother's back and shoulders while he waits for a doctor to arrive. Both a ruptured appendix and a bowel obstruction

At the Mae Tao Clinic in Thailand this baby receives free medical care for her burns, as her father, Zaw Win, and another child anxiously hope for her recovery.

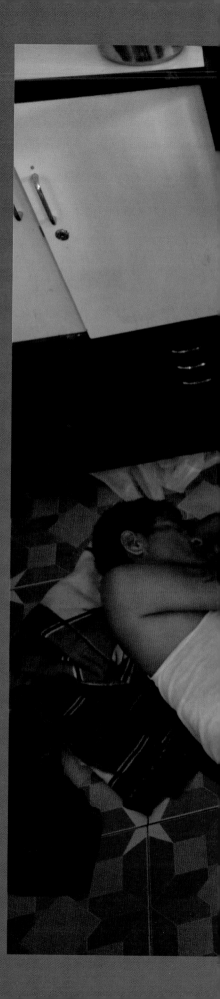

can prove fatal if not attended to within several days. But for this clinic, Soe Min would likely die.

A newborn lies with his mother and elder sibling while his father lies nearby on the floor. The boy was delivered at the clinic that day free of charge. His mother, Hla Kyi (39), and father, Palin Sein (39), had no place to go but heard that this clinic was free and that prospective mothers who suffer from hypertension should have their children at a clinic where doctors could monitor blood pressure during the delivery. Child and mother are doing fine. Luckily she made the right decision by coming to the clinic. Both parents are farmworkers who live day to day in near poverty to support their growing family. ■

Above: Another patient, Soe Min, 24, is experiencing extreme abdominal pain, possibly due to an intestinal block, as his little sister tries to comfort him. Right: Here, a healthy newborn has been delivered to his awaiting parents. Services such as these are rare in this part of Thailand.

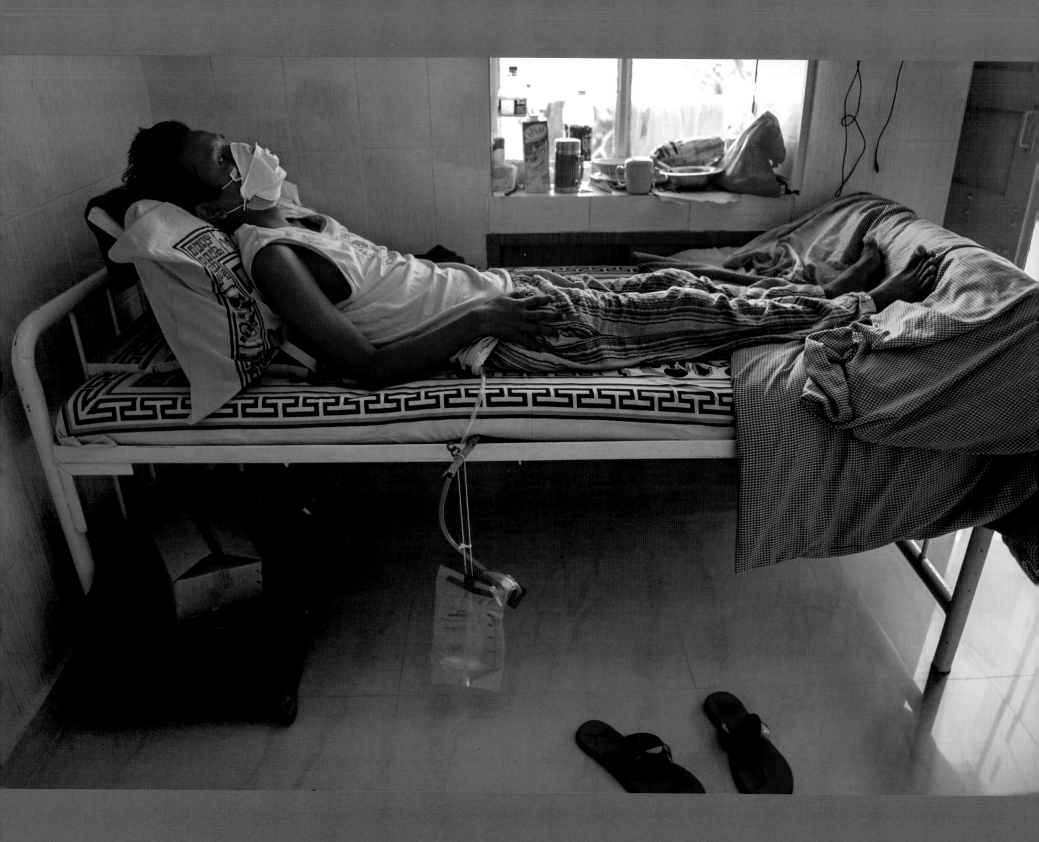

Tibetan Delek Hospital

At the Delek Hospital in northern India many of its patients are Tibetan refugees who are trying to survive tuberculosis. Tenzin Choney, 29, is one such refugee who could have died but for the services this hospital provides.

Although many people around the world believe that tuberculosis is largely a disease of the past, the truth is that each year TB still kills about 2 million people worldwide, 400,000 in India alone. The disease itself often attacks individuals between the ages of 15 and 45. Young adults who should be entering the most productive period of their lives must instead use this time to fight a disease that, if not treated properly, will kill them. As a result, the income they could have earned is denied them, and they and their families suffer from the loss of that income. This is, of course, very common and illustrates the cyclical relationship between one's health and poverty.

Tuberculosis used to be called "consumption." It was called this because the disease, if not treated quickly, can move from one's lungs to the bloodstream and then on to the kidneys and brain. Shortly thereafter, other organs are attacked and the body simply wastes away, or is "consumed" by the disease. Tuberculosis has also been thought to be an urban disease. That is because it is an airborne disease and those who are most likely to catch this illness often live in crowded urban settings where people live in close proximity to one another,

ventilation is poor, and where one person's sneeze or cough can easily become another's disease.

Tuberculosis is treatable with a series and combination of antibiotics that need to be administered properly over at least a six-month period. When not treated properly, or taken for an insufficient period of time, the disease can come back, and when it does it is often more resistant to further treatments and drugs. This type of tuberculosis has been called "multi-drug resistant" and is being found more and more throughout the world largely because many hospitals and medical service workers have not been trained properly on how to administer the drugs needed to combat this disease. So today more and more people are dying and hospitals are having to resort to more expensive and prolonged treatments to try and save those who are still alive.

As alluded to above, some people are more likely to acquire this disease than others. For example, in India, where there are more cases of tuberculosis than in any other country in the world, recent refugees from Tibet are, for a unique set of reasons, more likely to contract the disease than others in India. The reasons given for this anomaly are that

Liberia's Government Hospital: Repairing Women's Lives

At a special fistula unit at Liberia's government hospital in Tubmanburg, Liberia, come hundreds of girls and young women each year who have been cast out by their families and communities. They have been cast out because they live with a condition called obstetric fistulas, which are holes within the interior walls of their bodies connecting their birth canals with their bladders or rectums. This condition produces a strong odor and makes it impossible for them to continue to bear children, and in some communities in Africa and elsewhere those with the condition are thought of as undesirable, or as witches who need to be cast out.

This condition is actually quite common in parts of the world where medical services are rare and women attempt to deliver their children with little, if any, assistance from trained medical professionals. At this hospital, attempts are made to repair the interior walls of hundreds of these women each year. When such operations are successful, these women often return home to their respective villages to resume their lives, which in some cases have been lost to them for many years. This is the main reason why women travel great distances to come to the

hospital in Tubmanburg. In short, it is a chance to resume the life they once had.

This hospital's services are free for the rural women who come here. They are impoverished and likely would have never ended up with this condition but for their poverty and inability to access proper medical care when they needed it. Also fistula repairs often take repeated surgeries and require long-term stays in the hospital. This makes their hospitalization more expensive, and but for the hospital being free few could cover the cost of care.

Fistulas themselves most often occur when the delivery of a child goes terribly wrong, and no medical professional is available at the time of the child's birth. When this occurs, interior tissues are damaged or torn and the birth canal is left with an interior hole between organs. Sometimes, too, a child may, incorrectly, be pulled out of a woman's birth canal feet first, and in doing so the child's foot or leg may tear the interior walls of the woman's body. This not only can produce a fistula, but it often kills the child if the child is not already stillborn. Fistulas are also caused by violent sexual attacks on women, as well as by the rape of young

In Liberia's government hospital, Roseline Kella, 29, waits to receive surgery for a fistula from which she has been suffering for five years.

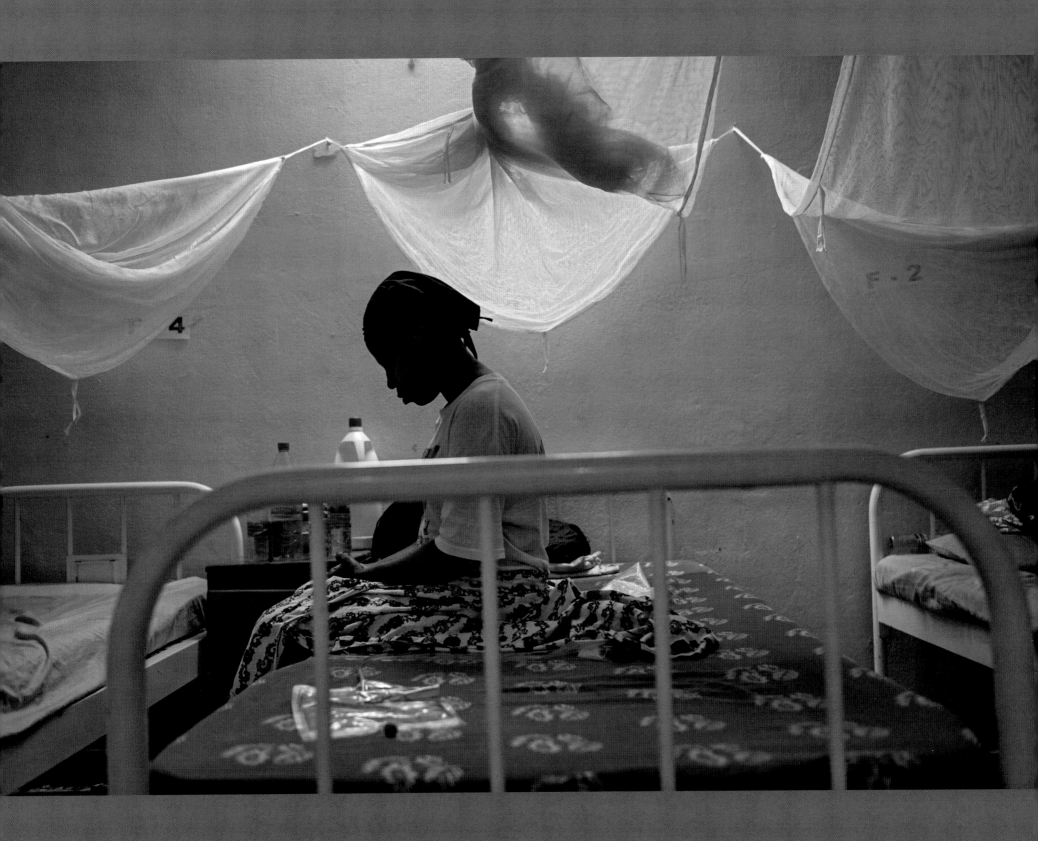

Left: In the forefront, Ester Cooper, 14, awaits her second fistula repair after her first failed. Behind her is Kpana Suno, 21, awaiting her third operation in the hope that this repair will work and she will be able to return to school.
Right: Unfortunately, these repairs are often not successful, as indicated by Mamie Kakula, who must sit on a bucket for hours every day because she can not control her bladder or bowels.

girls who are too small and fragile to engage in sexual intercourse.

As this profile opens we find Roseline Kella (29), one of the hospital patients, sitting on her bed. Roseline suffers from fistulas as a result of a child who died at birth some five years ago. She has since been abandoned by her parents and has left her 13-year-old daughter to be cared for by her sister. While waiting for her operation, she prays every day that her condition will be repaired and she will be allowed to return home.

In a nearby area of the hospital we find Ester Cooper. At 14 years of age she awaits her second operation after discovering that her first fistula

operation failed. Her family too has abandoned her and she likely developed her fistula when she attempted to give birth naturally at such a young age. Her child died. Behind her is Kpana Suno (21), whose baby was stillborn and in fact was found to be dead for three days before the child was removed from her body. Kpana is now waiting for her third operation with the hope of repairing her body so that one day she might return to school.

In the bathroom of the hospital Mamie Kakula sits on a bucket for six to eight hours a day. Her fistulas make it impossible for her to control urination as well as her bowel movements. Her first child died in 1992, and her second child caused

Barbara Alfred, 15, lives at an orphanage near Liberia's government hospital where she too suffers with a fistula after being raped by two men. She sleeps with no mattress because she cannot control her bladder and has soaked through too many.

"My only hope is that God will pity me." — Mamie Kakula

her condition. That child too died at birth, and she now has no children. Since her diagnosis, her family has abandoned her, and she has been living at the hospital for over a year getting a series of operations. She has lived with this condition for sixteen years. She says, "My only hope is that God will pity me."

Finally, Barbara Alfred, 15 years old, does not live at the government hospital in Tubmanburg. Instead she lives nearby at the Phebe Grey Memorial Orphanage in Monrovia, Liberia. Of the 108 children who live there, 10 children were raped prior to their arrival. Barbara was raped by two of her uncles and although both were arrested the rape left her with a fistula that makes it impossible for her to control her urine. She has been isolated from others at the orphanage and has been forced to sleep on only the metal springs of her bed because she has repeatedly soaked through her one mattress. In addition, Barbara suffers from malaria but does not have the funds necessary to get any medications for her illness, buy a mosquito net to protect her from mosquitoes, or pay for her travel to the government hospital in Tubmanburg to have her fistula repaired. ■

The Life of Jestina Koko

In Liberia lives a woman named Jestina KoKo. She is 25 years old and has struggled with a disability since the age of 3 when her parents noticed her legs simply did not work.

With a population of 4 million, 80 percent of whom live in poverty, Liberia is probably one of the worst places in the world to be disabled. That is because, as one of the poorest countries in the world, there exist few, if any, support services for those with disabilities. Moreover, Liberia has the second highest unemployment rate in the world, which from time to time has been estimated to be as high as 85 percent. In Liberia, most people live in an informal economy whereby bartering and other forms of trade for services are used simply to get by.

With all of this around her, Jestina gets through her day by walking about on her hands and arms and depends on them to lift and drag herself across the ground. She survives by begging, selling cookies that she makes herself, and washing the clothes of others. At the age of 12, she lost her mother and eventually was forced to move onto the streets, where she lived for some time. Some five years ago, Jestina gave birth to her daughter, Satta Quaye, but before her daughter was born, the child's father

Jestina Koko, 25, cannot walk. She drags herself about her home made of dirt and concrete in Liberia, where like many other developing countries of the world there is little if any assistance to those who are disabled, and so Jestina is left to fend for herself.

abandoned them. Satta, who often stays very close to her mother's side, tries to help when she can. Jestina would love nothing more than to have her child attend school rather than remain on the streets with her, but of course Jestina simply does not have the money to send her.

Today, and because of the goodwill of a neighbor, Jestina is allowed to sleep with her child in an extra room attached to the neighbor's dwelling. Jestina has almost no furniture and sleeps on the bare dirt floor with her daughter. What she prays for most is to be able to send her daughter to school and someday have their own room, a bed, and a wheelchair.

Above: For Jestina, the job she does to survive is the laundry of others. In doing so she drags herself about, hanging and washing clothes, while her daughter, Satta, 5, right, clings to her side. All they have is each other.

"What I pray for most is to someday send my daughter to school." — Jestina Koko (25)

Things are worse for them when the rain comes to Liberia, for it is during the rains that, because of Jestina's condition, she cannot drag herself through muddy streets or sit and beg outdoors. Baking cookies and washing clothes for others are also very difficult during the rainy season, for during those times of the year people with disabilities similar to hers find it very hard to survive.

Both Jestina and her daughter Satta also suffer from malaria. Malaria, of course, is quite common in this part of the world, particularly if one spends much time outdoors and has no access to something as simple as a mosquito net. With no salvation in sight for either Jestina or Satta, it is hard to say how their lives will end up. But, of course, this is the life that so many people with serious physical handicaps lead worldwide. Sometimes help can be so simple, such as in the case of some food, some bedding, or a wheelchair, and sometimes help can be overwhelming, particularly in countries where so many are poor and resources do not seem to be readily available to make a difference in their lives. ■

Jestina and Satta live in an extra room that a neighbor has kindly given them. It is what keeps them off the streets and allows Jestina to watch over her child, a child she hopes will someday go to school. However, her chances are slim at best.

and it is largely because of the odor that results and the woman's inability to have any more children that these women are often abandoned by their husbands and ostracized by their communities. Obstetric fistulas can also be the result of sexual violence.

In the developed world, where doctors or other medical professionals are usually available at the time of a child's birth, fistulas are quite rare because of the use of C-sections, and/or the ability to immediately repair such fistulas if and when they occur. Ironically, with poor women, however, the likelihood of requiring such surgery at the time of the birth of their child is heightened because of the fact that many poor women were malnourished as children and, as a result, their skeletal structure was stunted early in life. Hence, it is more common for them to have small pelvic areas, which cannot easily accommodate normal childbirth. At the same time, poor women have limited access to medical care, and fistulas that might result cannot be treated by way of either C-section or subsequent repair. Needless to say, poor women who suffer from this condition end up living very difficult lives, all the result of poverty and their inability to access needed medical care.

In conclusion, and when considering and addressing our global health problems, one must go beyond questions related to treatment and keep in mind the social and economic realities that exist in the world. For many, these realities suggest that, as a whole, we have not valued the lives of many and, as such, have simply not done enough to bring about health care to all. When quality health care is made available to all, people will live healthier, happier, and more productive and meaningful lives. This is something that everyone deserves and can benefit the world at large.

A Word About the Disabled of the World

Of all the world's poor, those who are most forgotten are the disabled. In many cases, they have been shunned by society, thought of as flawed individuals and not worth the time and energy it might take to include them within the mainstream of a particular country's working life. All this, in spite of the fact that depending on who you include within the category of the disabled they make up some 10–18 percent of our world's population, and so they are one of the world's largest minority groups, and one would think entitled to more rights and respect. The truth is, however, that only 25 percent of the world's countries provide for any legislation to protect the disabled from discrimination, or help in providing them with access to state facilities and/or programs specifically targeted to their needs.

Of the world's disabled population, 80 percent of them live in developing countries. They often are born with one of a variety of disabilities or become disabled as a result of an infection or a disease that often could have been prevented or cured if medical services had been available. Often, too, the disabled who live in poor countries become so as a result of an injury they have incurred at their place of work. In many cases the work the poor do is very dangerous and little if any resources are made available to compensate those injured for the disabilities they end up living with for the rest of their lives. Others who have become disabled have become so as a result of violence of one kind or another, or during war.

One of the immediate effects of living with a disability in the developing world is that it is very hard to find any kind of meaningful employment, and if the disability came on while one was young, often the condition would be used as an excuse to pull a child out of school. Hence, many disabled children in the developing world are illiterate and continue to be so as adults. In some countries, 80 percent of the disabled population are either illiterate or unemployed, or both.

Probably those individuals among the disabled who are most at risk are women and girls. It has been shown that they are far less likely to attend school than boys with greater disabilities, and are far more often than the general population to be raped, exploited, and/or sterilized. If you are a disabled woman, the truth is you have two strikes against you. If one couples this with

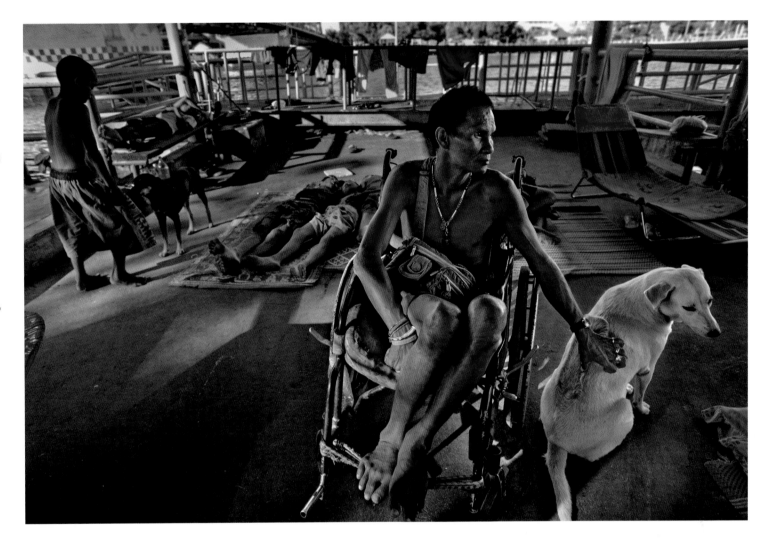

Manop Meksurya, 41, lives near the King Rama First Bridge in Bangkok, Thailand. He, along with some boys who share this area with him, are homeless. Manop has lived here for thirty-two years and recently contracted tuberculosis, and although relegated to a wheelchair and without any help from the government, he tries to help homeless boys who beg on the streets for that is what he did for many years. They band together to survive. As the oldest, he has become the boys' father figure.

poverty and the lack of family support or friends to reach out to, life can be very difficult indeed.

Another segment of the disabled population around the world who are particularly at high risk are those suffering from mental disabilities. This can be seen in even rich countries where those who are mentally ill can be found on the streets, homeless, and with little support from society. In poor countries, those with mental disabilities are among the most marginalized. They are often found living on roadsides, at railroad stations, on street corners, in alleyways, and in some countries often just become beggars. In these countries, where no governmental assistance for them exists, they live and die at the whim of those who may pass by and decide to help. Many of course die young and are taken away by state workers and their bodies disposed of. For those who are infected with some of the world's most loathsome diseases, such as leprosy or syphilis or AIDS, they are even more marginalized and, but for the work of saints, are nearly completely forgotten by the world at large. ■

A Way to Help

If you would like to help alleviate poverty and the suffering often associated with poverty, consider contacting one or more of the organizations below and ask how you can get involved.

CLINICIANS OF THE WORLD

Clinicians of the World provides specialized medical care, health education, and humanitarian aid to underserved people around the world regardless of culture, religion, or political affiliation. It works to improve health so that people can live productive lives. Its members believe that everyone in the world deserves an opportunity to live a healthy life.

Address: P.O. Box 116
            Rochester, MN 55903
Phone: (507) 208-4202
Email: help@cliniciansoftheworld.org
Website: www.cliniciansoftheworld.org

DOCTOR 2 DOCTOR

Doctor 2 Doctor provides volunteers who are medical professionals—physicians, psychologists, nurses, and others—who travel abroad to meet with their colleagues in other countries. They carry with them medications and books that are donated to the facilities they visit in an effort to help colleagues around the world help others.

Address: 1749 Martin Luther King Jr. Way
            Berkeley, CA 94709
Phone: (510) 548-5200
Email: info@d2d.org
Website: www.d2d.org

DOCTORS WITHOUT BORDERS

Doctors Without Borders provides medical aid in nearly sixty countries to people whose survival is threatened by violence, neglect, catastrophe, epidemics, malnutrition, or the lack of or exclusion from health care.

Address: 333 7th Avenue, 2nd Floor
            New York, NY 10001
Phone: (212) 679-6800
Email: See website for specific
            departments
Website: www.doctorswithoutborders.org

ESPERANÇA

Esperança provides hope and improves the health of families in the poorest communities of the world through sustainable disease prevention, education, and treatment.

Address: 1911 West Earll Drive
            Phoenix, AZ 85015
Phone: (602) 252-7772
Email: info@Esperanca.org
Website: www.esperanca.org

HEALTHCARE VOLUNTEER

HealthCare Volunteer provides a directory for anyone looking to volunteer their time and energy to health services and in doing so help those interested to find an appropriate volunteering opportunity that fits their wishes.

Address: 595 Loyola Drive
            Los Altos, CA 94024
Phone: N/A
Email: health@healthcarevolunteer.com
Website: www.healthcarevolunteer.com

HEART CARE INTERNATIONAL

Heart Care International provides heart surgeries and health care for children who suffer from congenital heart disease through a comprehensive array of volunteers, both lay and medical professionals. They also train host country medical professionals (doctors, nurses, administrative staff, etc.) in cutting-edge surgical, medical, palliative, and interventional care techniques such that local physicians will eventually be able to independently provide the same treatments to children in their home country.

Address: 139 East Putnam Avenue
            Greenwich, CT 06830
Phone: (203) 552-5343
Email: info@heartcareintl.org
Website: www.heartcareintl.org

MEDICAL MISSIONS

Medical Missions provides connections for people who wish to volunteer or seek employment with missions around the world who sponsor work in the delivery of medical care.

Address: 2655 Northwinds Pkwy
            Alpharetta, GA 30009
Phone: (866) 204-3200
Email: Form online
Website: www.medicalmissions.org

MEDICINE FOR PEACE

Medicine for Peace provides medical care and humanitarian assistance to children who are victims of war. MFP is a voluntary organization in which doctors, nurses, engineers, and dedicated individuals selflessly donate time, energy, and resources to achieve the goal of assisting children in need of medical attention in countries such as Iraq, Bosnia, and Haiti.

Address: 2732 Unicorn Lane NW
            Washington, DC 20015
Phone: (202) 441-4545
Email: medforpeace@aol.com
Website: www.medicineforpeace.org

MEDICINE IN ACTION

Medicine in Action provides avenues that serve to expose doctors and medical students to international opportunities in the field of global medical relief and service.

Address: 8101 Skyline Blvd
            Oakland, CA 94611
Phone: (510) 339-7579
Email: info@medicineinaction.org
Website: www.medicineinaction.org

MEDISEND

MediSend provides support for underresourced hospitals in developing countries with a multidimensional approach to improving community health. MediSend's mission includes education, training, technical support, and management technologies in Biomedical Equipment Repair, as well as the distribution of lifesaving medical supplies and biomedical equipment in long-term partnership with emergency relief programs.

Address: 9244 Markville Drive
             Dallas, TX 75243
Phone: (214) 575-5006
Email: info@medisend.org
Website: www.medisend.org

RESURGE INTERNATIONAL

ReSurge International provides free reconstructive surgeries for the poor and helps provide year-round medical assistance in underserved areas worldwide. In doing so, it restores the dreams of those with deformities and injuries, and influences the world by renewing the health of thousands of children and adults each year so they can go to school, provide for their families, and contribute to society. Its principal focus has been restoring the appearance of children with cleft lips or children who have been burned.

Address: 145 N. Wolfe Road
             Sunnyvale, CA 94086
Phone: (408) 737-8000
Email: info@resurge.org
Website: www.resurge.org

SMILE TRAIN

Smile Train provides free cleft surgery to hundreds of thousands of poor children in developing countries, trains doctors and medical professionals in over seventy-five countries, and treats the "whole child" with comprehensive, total rehabilitative care including speech therapy, general dentistry, and orthodontics.

Address: 41 Madison Ave., 28th Floor
             New York, NY 10010
Phone: (800) 932-9541
Email: info@smiletrain.org
Website: www.smiletrain.org

UMCOR

The United Methodist Committee on Relief (UMCOR) is a not-for-profit organization dedicated to alleviating human suffering around the globe. UMCOR's work reaches people in more than eighty countries, including the United States. It provides humanitarian relief when war, conflict, or natural disaster disrupts life to such an extent that communities are unable to recover on their own.

Address: 475 Riverside Drive, Room 1520
             New York, NY 10115
Phone: (800) 554-8583
Email: umcor@umcor.org
Website: www.umcor.org

VITAMIN ANGELS

Vitamin Angels provides private sector resources to advance the availability and access to micronutrients, especially vitamin A, for newborns, infants, and children in need around the world. Vitamin A improves the immunity system of children and helps prevent blindness. It is widely used in the developed world to reduce child mortality, especially those under the age of five. Such vitamins are provided free or at very low cost.

Address: P.O. Box 4490
             Santa Barbara, CA 93140
Phone: (805) 564-8400
Email: info@vitaminangels.org
Website: www.vitaminangels.org

WHEELCHAIR FOUNDATION

Wheelchair Foundation provides a free wheelchair to every child, teen, and adult in the world who needs one but cannot afford one. Wheelchair Foundation also raises awareness of the needs and abilities of people with physical disabilities, promotes the joy of giving, and creates global friendship.

Address: 3820 Blackhawk Road
             Danville, CA 94506
Phone: (877) 378-3839
Email: info@wheelchairfoundation.org
Website: www.wheelchairfoundation.org

WORLD CATARACT FOUNDATION

World Cataract Foundation provides free cataract surgery to people in twenty-five countries with the goal of eliminating cataract blindness worldwide.

Address: 6463 Poplar, Suite 101
             Memphis, TN 38119
Phone: (901) 379-0405
Email: See form on website
Website: www.worldcataract.org

WORLDWIDE FISTULA FUND

Worldwide Fistula Fund provides medical treatment for women suffering from obstetrical fistulas. WFF also promotes excellent training for fistula surgeons as well as helps advocate for the unmet health needs of women suffering from this condition as well as encourages scientific research in fistula treatment and prevention.

Address: 1100 E. Woodfield Road, Suite 350
             Schaumburg, IL 60173
Phone: (847) 592-2438
Email: info@wffund.org
Website: www.worldwidefistulafund.org

Note: For more information on how to get involved in assisting in the medical needs of the poor, please check out these directories:

http://dir.yahoo.com/Health/Medicine/
Organizations/International_Relief_and_
Development/?o=a

The Women Who Save the World

It is, of course, impossible to generalize about all the women of the world. Some live fairly privileged lives and for them life can be quite different than for the women who live in poverty. However, with regard to women in general, one thing that can be said is that, collectively, women make up the largest percentage of people who live in poverty or near poverty worldwide. In fact, of the more than 2 billion people who can easily be considered to be poor on the planet, nearly two thirds of them are women or girls. This chapter is about them.

At the outset, let us try to clear up one myth that seems to be broadly held by many of us, and this is that there are more women on earth than men. The truth is just the opposite. The basis of this belief seems to be driven by two facts. First, females live longer than males, about four years longer. With the average life expectancy of males worldwide at 66 years of age and the average life expectancy for females at 70 years of age, it is with good reason that one believes there are more females than males. They simply live longer.

Second, most people believe that, during times of war, more men die than women. This, of course, reduces the number of males as opposed to females worldwide. Although true, this is changing because wars have changed.

Now during wartime it is not unusual for more civilians to be killed than soldiers, and when civilians die many are women and children. In spite of this, however, and for reasons that we will discuss below, at last count there were 57 million more males on earth than females. Regardless of their fewer numbers, however, it can easily be said that women contribute more than their fair share to the human experience, and what they do for the world and humankind in general is immeasurable.

In short, they give birth to our children, often rear them exclusively, feed and nurture our families and extended families, work long hours, care for aging family members, and labor almost continuously to keep families intact, regardless of what seems to be going on around them. Additionally, women not only take care of our families but are responsible for 60 to 80 percent of food production in the developing world. They care for livestock, they often spend long hours carrying water, food, and fuel to wash, feed, and maintain their families, and when not the sole income source for their family often provide for a secondary income stream, which can, in some cases, keep their family out of poverty and provide their children with opportunities that they themselves never had. Women are also routinely sit by the side of a sick child, disabled husband, or dying elder at their times of greatest need. For all of this, women have yet to be treated fairly all over the world, and in nearly all countries they face various kinds of discrimination, hardship, and violence, some of which starts before they are even born.

Women at their time of birth
Although I suspect that Mother Nature has a good reason for doing this, she herself discriminates against females at their time of birth, because for every 100 girls born 105 to 106 boys are born. Nevertheless, even with this natural inclination toward boys in the world's birthrate, the world's desire for boys has yet to be satisfied, for in all but some developed countries boys are desired over girls by parents and families. A couple of examples of how boys are favored over girls, even before their birth, can be found by examining the practical effects of China's 1979 effort to limit population growth and promote its "one child per family" policy among the citizenry as well as how India and other countries in Southeast Asia treat the birth of girl children as opposed to boys. It is common for families in this area of the world to prefer boys and work toward selecting the gender of their child before their child is born. They do so by means of selective abortions. This has been made possible because of advances in technology whereby today prospective parents, even in less developed countries, are able to make use of ultrasound procedures to find out the gender of their developing fetus. In doing so, if it is determined that the child will likely be a girl, the child is aborted. Moreover, if the family already has one girl and it is determined that the second child will also be a girl, that child will be aborted with even more frequency. This is done in spite of the fact that in many parts of Southeast Asia the act of using this technology for the purposes of determining gender or informing parents about the gender of the developing fetus is illegal. However, when parents' desire for a boy child is so great, a way can always be found to circumvent, if not ignore, the law.

In China, boys are favored over girls because they will carry on the family name and, to some extent, the family assets. Knowing this, and knowing that only one child per family is allowed by the government, prospective parents in China very much hope for a boy for he may represent the only opportunity to carry on the family's name to the next generation.

In India, the practice of applying ultrasound to selectively abort children is used as a means to avoid paying dowries. This is done in spite of the fact that it has been illegal to use ultrasound devises to determine the gender of a child in India since 1998. Indian families who have girls often must, upon their marriage, pay a dowry to their daughter's husband or her in-laws as a condition of the marriage. The historical reason for dowries was that because women provided far less income to a family throughout the marriage, a dowry was given to her husband or his family in order to better equalize the wife's contribution to the marriage. Here, too, and in spite of the fact that demanding dowries is also illegal in India, and has been since 1961, dowries are still very common to the culture and remain expected of many families, rich or poor.

These dowries are very difficult on the poor, particularly when a family may have several girls in line for marriage. In practice, this makes girls far more of a liability than boys and imposes an economic hardship on impoverished families who cannot afford to meet the obligations of the dowry system. Also, when girls and young women marry in India, whatever income they might have been providing their parents moves to their new husband and his family. As a result, poor families often work to select boys over girls before their birth and do so by seeking abortions to put a quick end to this problem. These abortions account for many of the millions performed in India each year.

This practice of selecting boys over girls has been going on throughout China, India, and Southeast Asia for the past thirty years, if not longer, and as a result today China alone is missing 50 million females. That is to say that if natural forces were left in place, there would be 50 million more females in China today. Because of this phenomenon, Chinese and Asian men in general have now been experiencing some difficulty finding life partners. Moreover, throughout India and Southeast Asia, the situation is even worse, and it has now been estimated that in this part of the world there are between 100 and 163 million missing females. In some cases, these were females who were sent off to other countries to be adopted, but in most cases these were females never born simply because of policies and economics that didn't favor their existence. Because nearly half of the world's population lives in China, India and Southeast Asia, this imbalance has begun to affect the rest of the world and in large part has begun to create the world's present imbalance in gender. The only saving grace that may be said about this is that the worldwide

imbalance is concentrated among the younger age groups and diminishes incrementally as women get older. In fact, by age 50, women outnumber men. This is true because of the fact that women do live longer than men. Futurists tell us, however, that if these trends continue there will be more violent crime and more human trafficking of women to provide for the needs of men in areas of the world that will be experiencing the greatest shortage of women. More women, too, will be sold as brides to men because of the law of supply and demand and families will eventually resort to buying wives for their sons who find it difficult to find life partners. In some areas of the world, this is already happening. All of this because of the discrimination that is faced by females even before they are born.

Note: in some regions of the world female infanticide accounts for a very large number of the world's missing females. Under these circumstances infants, often less than a week old, are killed for some of the same reasons mentioned above, and although no one knows for sure how often this occurs it has been estimated that in some cases such practices may account for as many as one third of that locale's missing females. Countries that have been found to practice female infanticide are Pakistan, India, Bangladesh, China, South Korea, Singapore, and Taiwan as well as some parts of Africa. In Pakistan, the practice has even been used to do away with illegitimate children. Overall, however, nine out of every ten infants killed for these reasons are girls.

When women are young

When women are young they continue to face discrimination, sometimes in subtle ways, but these practices are certainly most common among the world's poor. For example, impoverished girls are less likely to get the medical care they need simply because their lives are not as valued as those of boys. Hence, when there is a limited amount of money, a limited amount of time, or limited access to medical care, it is usually a young girl's needs that are put in abeyance. This is also true with food. A disproportionate number of the malnourished children in the world are girls. They are the last to eat and when a family is facing a food shortage, they simply never get enough. As a result, they grow up stunted, have grave difficulties bearing children, and often experience ancillary problems throughout their life. (See chapter 4.)

Young girls are often last to go to school. It is because their services are often required at home to help their mothers and care for younger children. They also tend to the gathering of water, fuel, and food and look after the overall needs of the family. It has been estimated that of the 15 million school age children who are not attending primary school, nearly 60 percent of them are girls and these numbers only worsen as children move on to secondary school because it is then when a girl's services are often needed most. Many girls are pulled out of school at around age ten to work and help the family. At many schools that serve the extreme poor, few provisions are made to protect young girls' privacy as they get older and they are often required to use open toilets with boys. Often, they are sexually harassed and teased, making the school experience quite difficult and so they simply drop out. Because of all of this, two thirds of the nearly one billion adults in the world who are illiterate are women. This, of course, affects their ability to acquire any kind of high status or make incomes equal to adult males. It also places them at a lifelong economic disadvantage and accounts for one of the main reasons why women and children are the poorest people on earth.

Adolescent girls

In many parts of the developing world another consequence of being a girl is that she will likely marry young. In many cases, these are forced marriages. In fact, in some countries, it is not unusual for girls to be sold off and married to older men even before the age of ten. Girls are sometimes encouraged to marry young when poor families can no longer afford to care for them or when there is some kind of economic benefit associated with

the marriage. In some cultures, if a young girl has been raped, her family may no longer want her, and marriage, if even possible, may be her only option. This is true particularly if she is illiterate and has no means of support. It is no wonder that in developing countries around the world we find that so many girls are married (either legally or commonly) before they turn 18 years of age. All told, there exists more than 50 million young brides in the world today.

Some of the consequences experienced by these young brides include the likelihood that they will have many children, work long hours, never finish school, live in poverty and die young. As an illustration of this, today women throughout the world have an average of 2.5 children. However, women in the developing world who marry young have five or more children. In poor families, having many children is encouraged because it will be the children who will care for the parents as the parents age. This is particularly important in countries that do not provide for any kind of social security or social safety net for the poor. It is in these countries that children provide for that security for the elderly. In many parts of the world, too, having many children doesn't necessarily guarantee that they will survive to adulthood, and so the poor often have more children than they can afford and hope that most will survive and provide for them when they age. It is, of course, the women of the developing world that bear the burden of birthing and rearing these children.

Another challenge associated with early marriage and childbirth is that young women do not always have the ability to access appropriate medical care and, as discussed in chapter 4, young women who have children while they themselves are technically still children are at the greatest risk of not surviving childbirth. This is particularly true in the developing world where young women have often been malnourished since birth and as a result are stunted in size. Their bodies are simply not ready to bear children. If one couples this with the fact that they often give birth without any kind of skilled nursing or medical care, it is

Text continues on page 156

Arranged marriages are quite common in certain areas of the world. Here a 14-year-old girl in Bangladesh, sitting next to her soon to be husband, was sold off by her family in the hopes that it would bring her a better life. For young girls like her, often it does not.

The Kayayo Girls of Ghana

They are called the Kayayo Girls of Ghana, also known as the "porter girls." They have come to an area of Accra, Ghana's capital city, from the northern part of the country largely because it is in the north where poverty is at its worst. With little chance to earn a living in the rural areas of northern Ghana, these girls, often as young as 10 to 12, come in the thousands to the city to try to eke out something of a living for themselves. Sometimes they come because they are pregnant and believe that because they have no husbands they will not be accepted by their village.

Many Kayayo Girls live in an area of Accra that is part of the city dump and, because they can only afford to live there, they are often treated poorly by others and are sometimes accosted on the streets where they work. They sleep on the floors of makeshift shacks, often with their children, and with as many as eighteen girls to a room. They get up at 3 A.M. in order to get to the city market by 4 A.M. where they wait to help wealthier people get their produce home to their families. In doing so, they place vegetables and fruits on their head, strap their children to their backs, and sometimes walk very long distances,

In a slum in the capital city of Accra, in Ghana, West Africa, family members prepare for the day's work either collecting waste or serving as porters for the wealthier residents of this city. Their makeshift shacks serve as their only home, sometimes ten to twenty people in a room. It is all they can afford.

with very heavy loads, for very little money. They do so in order to pay their rent, buy some food for themselves and their children, and aquire whatever meager possessions they may need in the hopes of bringing about a better life, if not for themselves then for their children.

One such young woman who does this kind of work goes by the name of Barchisu (19). On any given day one can find her carrying a heavy load of bananas with her son, Yusif (1), strapped to her back, at a market in Accra. On a good day, Barchisu can make up to 5 Ghanaian cedi, or about $3.30, but on other days she may make nothing at all. She has been living the life of a Kayayo Girl in Accra for five years. She says that her parents could no longer take care of her, for they had no money. She also believes her life will

Right: In addition to carrying bananas, sometimes with their children strapped to their back, Kayayo Girls, left, also take care of their own needs and those of their family, while at the same time trying to get enough sleep in order to survive another day.

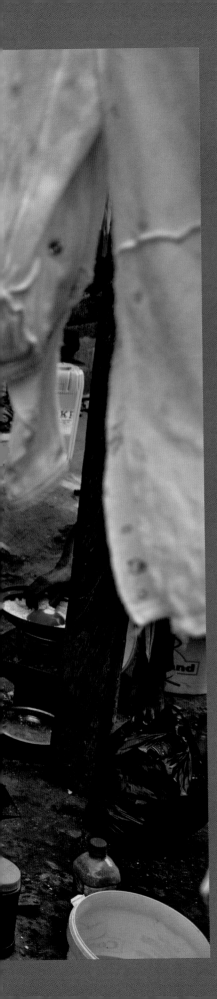

Left: In order to survive, Kayayo Girls live in communal settings that require the least amount of rent, often near or on top of the city dump, above.

never change because of her lack of education and the fact that she makes so little money. She worries, too, about whether the government will push her out of a shack she sleeps in with other Kayayo Girls at the city dump. She is proud, however, that she has been able to feed herself, pay her hospital bill, and pay for bath and toilet services. She also buys herself some palm oil that she uses after bathing but says that she can never get married because she needs to focus on her life and work hard if she wants to see her son go to school someday.

On Sundays Barchisu does laundry. Sometimes she washes clothes for others, and makes a little extra money that way, but often it is just her work

as a Kayayo Girl and her time with her child that occupies most of her life. This is true for nearly all Kayayo Girls who take up this work with their small children by their sides.

Amina (12) has been living on the streets of Accra for the past two years. For some time she has been sick with headaches, vomiting, cold chills, and sweating. She has no family in Accra to help her and sits at the banana market where she works as a Kayayo Girl. On some days, she cries from the pain in her head. She is small and quite frail, and it is often difficult for her to carry heavy loads so she makes far less than other girls. The symptoms Amina is experiencing are likely related to malaria. She says, "I work outside and a lot of mosquitoes bite me." Since malaria is quite prevalent in this part of Africa, that would explain her symptoms.

When she was 10, Amina came from northern Ghana on a truck that was carrying bananas. Her parents were farmers and because of problems she experienced at home she decided to run away. Today, however, she wants nothing more than to return to her family but neither she nor her family has the funds or the courage to make the trip. If she tries to make the trip alone, she is afraid that someone will threaten her, beat her, rape her, or steal her money. These kinds of incidents are not unusual in this part of the world. Often she cries, and says, "I just want to go home." The little money she has should likely go toward malaria medicine, but with few adults to advise her she remains at a loss for what to do.

It's a Sunday and many of the Kayayo Girls are tending to their children. Meryi (17) has worked

with the Kayayo Girls for two years and today she is visiting with them. She says the work was exhausting and she could never make enough money. Recently she started working with an aunt who lives some miles away and makes rice and beans to sell at the market, but still she struggles to survive. Meryi originally came to Accra because she had no money and her father was old and could not work. Her mother too had no job, so there was little future for her at home working the fields in the agricultural areas of the country. When asked if she is happy, she says "No, I am not happy. I'm suffering. If I could get money, I would go back to my village and help my family. Maybe I would buy a business

Far left: Amina, 12, ponders her life as a porter girl and cries from the pain associated with malaria.
Above: Meryi, 17, and her child (center) return to visit the women she once worked with, as they prepare dinner.

"I am not happy. I am suffering. If I could get money, I would go back to my village and help my family." — Meryi (17)

Kandi, 25, feeds her son Baba, 4, who suffers from malaria. Between her life of work and her son's need for care, she has little time for herself, but nothing is more clear here than a mother's love.

and send my boy to school." The baby's father pays no support. She does not know what will happen to her and her child.

More than anything else, what can be said about the Kayayo Girls of Ghana is that they work very hard for very little and spend most of their lives caring for their children and families. It is actually what many of the poorest women on earth spend their lives doing. Kandi (25) is a very good example of the women of the world who do this as she cares and feeds her sick son, Baba (4). He has diarrhea, has been vomiting, and has a headache that doesn't go away.

Kandi, too, came from the northern regions of Ghana about four years ago around the time she was getting ready to give birth to Baba. Although she is extremely poor and has never found any governmental agency or nongovernmental organization that might be willing to help her, she proceeds with the tenacity often found in mothers everywhere to try to make a life for herself and her child. This is true in spite of the fact that all she possesses can be found in a bucket by her side. Hopefully her son will survive this illness. She certainly deserves that much. ■

A Brothel in Bangladesh

In the city of Jessore, Bangladesh, we found one of the thousands upon thousands of brothels that are located throughout the world in both rich and poor countries alike. Here the brothel is called Marwari Mandir. It is home to sex workers, both young and old, who each day sell their bodies for very little money. In fact, over the course of a day, and after attending to many clients, sex workers at this brothel are lucky to make 400 to 600 taka ($5–$8).

Bangladesh is a country where nearly half of its citizens live in poverty, and when compared to its neighbors, namely India, Pakistan, and Sri Lanka, it provides its people with an even lower standard of living and only the most minimal access to basic services. This is one of the reasons why some women turn to this occupation. It is, however, an occupation that has many risks and few rewards.

The women at the Marwari Mandir brothel keep very little, if any, of the money they earn. Instead, whatever they receive is turned over to their respective "mothers" (these are the madams who often are not related to the sex worker by blood, but instead informally adopt young girls, teach them the trade, have them work, and in return provide them with food and shelter). The "mothers" of the brothel

also use the funds they receive to pay for electricity, local police protection (bribes), and any other additional security that might be necessary to help keep their girls safe.

The young girls who live at the brothel often stay for many years because it becomes their home and the other workers become their family. In fact, many girls and women have children there, grow old, and eventually become "mothers" themselves to young girls who are brought to the brothel and adopted by them in the same way they may have been adopted themselves. Often, too, it is sometimes the children of the prostitutes who are eventually taken into the brothel and follow in their mothers' footsteps. Other young girls are found on the street, abducted by sex traffickers, or are either knowingly or inadvertently sold into this way of life by impoverished parents. Most young girls who work at brothels are quite secretive about their age since in Bangladesh they are not legally allowed to enter into this line of work until they are at least 18 years of age.

Anema (45) is known as one of the madams or "mothers" of the girls and lives at the Marwari Mandir brothel. She lives in a room surrounded by

Anema, 45, sits in her room in the brothel where she once worked. Now she works as a "mother," caring for the girls who service men and relying on them to support her as she is no longer as desirable as when she was young.

Left: Golapy, one of the brothel's youngest prostitutes, stands by the doorway as she waits for her first client of the day. Right: Labone, 27, takes a moment to hold her young daughter Nupur, I, who was fathered by a client, before she has to return to her evening's work.

images of herself taken when she was young. At this point in her life, however, few clients want her so she relies on girls and younger women to support her as she lives out her years at the brothel.

One of those younger workers is a girl named Golapy who each morning waits by the entrance to the brothel for her first client of the day. Golapy is in fact quite young, likely one of the youngest workers at the brothel. When girls appear young, it can raise questions as to their age, so at this brothel, young prostitutes take steroids, which make them look older, and at the same time the steroids make them gain weight, which in Bangladesh men find desirable.

Many of the women at the brothel have children, as evidenced by Labone (27) who stands in the battered doorway to her room with her daughter Nupur (I). She will shortly turn over the responsibility of caring for her daughter to one of the "mothers" at the brothel as she prepares for her evening's work. Labone suffers from hepatitis and has contracted AIDS. It is, of course, hard to know how long she will survive and difficult to say what will happen to her daughter. Nupur will more than likely remain at the brothel and eventually continue in her mother's footsteps when her mother can no longer work and Nupur becomes of age, whenever that might be.

Nupur, another young worker at the brothel, says she is 20 years old. She has been at the brothel for three years. Each day she puts on her makeup and gets ready for clients that may happen to come to the front door. She is carrying the hepatitis B virus and is very sick. She has to work because her "mother" wants the money. At some point, however, she will have to ask if she can use some of her money to get the medical care she needs and take some time off to rest. Hepatitis B can be a chronic condition, but with proper treatment and rest her symptoms will go away and she can return to work. At that point, the yellow in her eyes may begin to dissipate. Nupur has never been tested for the HIV virus, but far too often sex workers who have hepatitis have contracted AIDS as well.

Each day at the Marwari Mandir brothel, sex workers take turns encouraging prospective clients to enter the brothel and choose from one of the several waiting girls and women. Sometimes the clients at the brothels are young men seeking their first sexual encounter. Premarital sex is frowned upon in Bangladesh and women who have had sex prior to marriage have difficulty finding a husband, so men resort to prostitutes for this reason. Young men are often preferred by sex workers for they are naive, inexperienced, and usually bring with them little threat of violence. Often, too, they have not learned how to bargain and in some cases may pay more for services than do older men. Nevertheless, while bargaining is taking place at the front door of the brothel, Rozena (26) awaits at the rear entrance for customers who may wish to remain more discreet and have previously worked out a

price for services. On any given day it is hard to say who or how many men may come calling.

This way of life can last for many years unless the girls and women contract AIDS or another communicable disease, which may shorten their working life, if not extinguish it. Sometimes, too, sex workers may have an encounter with a client that goes terribly wrong and these women are later found injured or dead. One such sex worker and victim of this kind of violence is named Pinky who, on some days, and as a result of being beaten, must take some extra time in applying her makeup in order to cover a black eye she received from a client the night before. This is one of the occupational hazards of the job these young

Far left: Nupur, 20, has contracted hepatitis B, indicated by the color of her eyes, likely as a result of her work.
Above: Brothel workers encourage a young prospective client to enter, hoping that due to his inexperience he might be persuaded to pay more than what is customary for services.

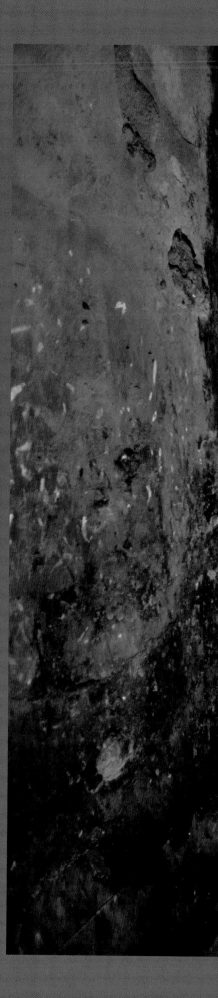

women endure throughout much of their lives. In some cases, the violence they experience can end their careers. Of course, all of the women stay close to one another and if there is any suspicion that a client may become violent, they come to each other's assistance. Nevertheless, often things happen quite quickly and it is a risk they all live with day in and day out. Prostitutes in Bangladesh almost never marry for there are few men in this part of the world who would choose a woman who has earned her living in this manner. In Bangladesh, as well as many other countries, this has been a way of life for centuries, often driven by poverty, exploitation, abuse, and the need to survive. ■

Above: Brothel worker Pinky prepares for another day's work using makeup to cover a black eye she received from a client. For many of these women it's an occupational hazard they endure.

Right: Rozena, 26, waits at the back door for clients that wish to remain anonymous.

Mrs. Bujor: A Grandmother's Love

Women who spend their later years caring for their grandchildren can be found all over the world. For the poor of the world, however, it is a service that is often provided under very difficult circumstances and not without a great deal of hardship, on both the grandmothers and the grandchildren they undertake to raise. Take, for example, the life of Viorica Bujor, who lives in the village of Fintinita, Moldova, in eastern Europe and who cares for her grandchildren.

Viorica Bujor is 78 years old. She lives in a home that has no electricity, no toilet facilities, dirt floors, and windows with broken glass. After her daughter died several years ago when, as she says, "a doctor made a mistake," she was left to take care of her three grandchildren, two girls and a boy. They live only on her pension, which amounts to 700 lei or about $58 U.S. a month. With that money, she buys potatoes and beans to feed herself and her grandchildren. It is something she has been doing for years.

In a room adjacent to where she cooks and sleeps, she keeps four chickens and a goose. It is nearly all she owns in the world. The birds produce food for the family. Her days

In her home in Moldova, Viorica Bujor, 78, holds two goose eggs that will make up a significant part of her grandchildren's dinner. For twelve years this family has lived in a house with no electricity, broken windows, and no heat.

"I take care of my grand-children after my daughter died because a doctor made a mistake." — Viorica Bujor (78)

Above: The socks worn by Viorica hardly keep out the bitter cold, but it is all she has.
Far right: Andrei, 18, Viorica's grandchild who is mentally disabled, is warming his bed to help put off the evening's cold.

consists of burning wood in her stove to stay warm throughout much of the year and cooking whatever she can gather to eat and feed her grandchildren. She also works with others in her village to try and keep her grandchildren in school and help them in whatever way she can to give them a chance at a better life.

Viorica's oldest grandchild, Ana Gobati (19), is mentally disabled and recently gave birth to a child. Ana had to move to a monastery for the sake of the infant, because it would have been impossible for her to keep such a young child in good health in the home in which they live. Andrei, her 18-year-old grandson, works hard every day to help his

grandmother since she broke her leg some years ago and working around the house causes her a great deal of pain.

Andrei helps by cutting wood, lighting fires in the stove, feeding the birds, and working in the garden. Although he too is mentally disabled, he recently graduated from a school for children with special educational needs. He loves math and hopes to do something important with his life someday. In the winter he lights a fire under his bed to keep warm. This is something that is done in this part of the world by the poor in order to better get through the cold nights.

Also during the winter months the family often does not bathe, because with little heat and little clothing they might freeze. Moreover they must wear the same clothing for months. Washing clothes is difficult in Moldova because they will not dry outdoors during the short, cold winter days. As one can see from Mrs. Bujor's well-worn socks, life has been extremely difficult, but caring for her grandchildren is what she will do until she can no more. Again, this is what so many women do all over the world. So many unsung heroes. ■

the brothel owners, and at these places of business the children of prostitutes are often used to better ensure that their mothers will not run off and leave the establishment.

This is not to suggest that prostitution in and of itself necessarily victimizes women. Some women "freely" choose this type of work, but in most cases throughout the impoverished world, too many women have entered this world as children because of poverty or the wrongdoing of another, and even if they later remain prostitutes their decision to do so can never be considered of their own doing because of the victimization that occurred when they were still children. According to international law, girls are considered children up until they reach the age of 18. Women too who have been deceived or forced into prostitution are victims as well.

Yet another kind of violence that women today still endure relates to dowries, as mentioned earlier in the chapter. This type of violence has been called "dowry killings," or "bride burnings," and is fairly common in India. When families who have been promised dowries are not paid those dowries, they sometimes retaliate by killing the young woman who recently entered into their family through marriage and, in their view, owes them the dowry. Often the killing is done by her new husband. Often too it is made to look like an accident whereby the recent bride is found burned to death in the kitchen of her home and claims are made about a kitchen fire that simply got out of hand. India has 50,000 such deaths a year. In some cases women are killed even after they paid their dowry so that their husbands can remarry and possibly collect a second dowry from a new wife/victim. In Bangladesh, women have been attacked with acid and disfigured or blinded for failing to pay their dowry or for disobeying their husbands. Again, and as noted above, although demanding a dowry has been against the law in India for some fifty years, the custom seems to continue over the government's attempts to prosecute those who have perpetrated these crimes against women.

It is ironic that for all the good that women do, they continue to face so much hardship, discrimination, pain, and suffering, frequently encompassing the entirety of their lives. Of course, there are no good reasons for any of this, only good reasons for bringing it to an end. ■

Women throughout the world, regardless of their age, are often first in line to care for those who cannot yet care for themselves. Here an impoverished young woman in northern India, who is undernourished herself, brings two babies suffering from malnutrition to a clinic for help.

CHAPTER SIX

Children at Work

Children throughout the world frequently work to help support their families. In some cases, they give up their chance at school to do what they can to help. This boy of 6, battered by rain, works for his father herding cows in Ghana, West Africa. He dreams of attending school someday but likely will never get there.

No one really knows how many children worldwide give up a large part of their growing-up years to work, but many have taken fairly good guesses. Of course, the numbers vary depending on who is counting and what one might consider "a child" or what one might consider "work." As to the definition of a child, that part is easy, for under international law, namely the International Convention on the Rights of the Child, a child is any human being below 18 years of age unless the local law applicable to the child places his or her age of majority at an earlier age. As to what is "work" (or that which might be considered "child labor"), that definition is somewhat more difficult. Nevertheless, this chapter will give the reader a better sense as to what might be acceptable for children to do in the way of work and what might be more problematic, if not outright unlawful. Remember, numbers alone can never tell the full story of the millions upon millions of children who work day in and day out throughout the world, and part of the problem associated with coming up with accurate figures as to the numbers of children who work is that we are now only beginning to come to a consensus as to what defines child labor.

The type of work children do worldwide varies greatly but depends on the climate, the area of the world in which they live, the type of work their parents

The Children Who Farm

As noted in the text in this chapter, probably the most common type of work that children do around the world is farming, much of which is done in Africa. There, and elsewhere, children usually farm on the land owned by their parents but also on land owned by others. As a result of their labor children help support their families by either acquiring some of the crops that they harvest or selling some of the crop and getting the money they and their families need to simply survive.

In a village called Kabiti, north of Nkwanta in Ghana, live seven children (two sisters and five brothers) all of whom work each day to plant and harvest yams that the family eats and, in a good year, sells at market. Kwame Safew (6) and Kwame Gafaru (7) go off to work at about 7 A.M. with their homemade hoes to clear weeds and give the yams they have planted an opportunity to grow. At 7, Kwame Gafaru has already been doing this work for three years. He and his brothers do this with little food in their bellies, no shoes on their feet, and the threat of punishment if they come home too early.

This year, things look very bad for their family. There has been little rain, and many of the seeds

Far left: Kwame Gafaru, 7, left, and his brother Kwame Safew, 6, right, begin their day's work by walking through the bush in Ghana to join their siblings on their father's yam farm.
Left: They often work the farm without shoes or protective gear.

they have planted have not germinated at the rate in which they hoped. When this occurs, they are forced to survive on last year's harvest, which by now has little nutritional value, and during some periods of the season they go days without any food at all. It is now August, and ordinarily harvest would have occurred in July, but still the yams have not ripened, and this year few may ripen at all. Foreseeing that this might happen, the children over the course of

"If I could go to school, I would. My father is a farmer, my mother is a farmer, but I don't want to be a farmer."

— Kwame Safew (6)

Above: Kwame Domminic, 42, watches over his children as they clear weeds. Far right: Kwame Joshua, 6, suffers from malaria but still must work to help his family, for it is in part his labor that helps keep them alive.

previous months have planted rice and corn, but this too is completely dry. In a good year, they would have been able to sell at least one third of their crop, but because of the ways of nature this year they will have no money and barely enough to eat.

All the members of this family have malaria except a recent child who is only a year old. With this year's crop failure, they will have no emergency money, no money for medicine, clothing, or even shoes. Shoes are important but they are not ordinarily something they have money to buy, and as a result Kwame Safew's feet are weathered and often cut and open to infections. The boys work

together to clear small plots of land where they can plant their crops. It is not unusual for them to work nearly all day, taking only a short break in midday because of the sweltering heat. They wish that they could go to school, but the family has absolutely no money to pay school fees, and their labor is needed in the fields.

The boys' father, Kwame Domminic (42), watches over them as they work. He assists them from time to time, while remaining alert for snakes and animals that can harm them at any given moment. The children who work for the family range in age from 5 to 11. It is work they do every day without much thanks or any kind of reward, other than knowing that if they did not work they would likely not survive. When asked about his life, Kwame Safew said, "I am poor and haven't got enough education. If I could go to school, I would. My father is a farmer, my mother is a farmer, but I don't want to be a farmer. I want to go to school. With no rain, our crops won't grow. We will get food to eat, but not to sell. This will be a hard year. Only if my father gets support will life change." ∎

A Blind Child

Found within a constant swirl of people outside a mosque in New Delhi sits a blind girl in a wheelchair named Hunupa Begum. She is 13 years old and has been blind for ten years. She is also her family's sole means of support.

Her mother, Manora Begum (35), believes that doctors could have saved her eyesight, but she had no money and by the time anyone would see her daughter it was too late. So today, in the midst of thousands of people and a swarm of trucks and vehicles of all kinds, each day Hunupa begs for enough money to buy some food to feed her mother and younger brother, Hajimudin Sheikh, age 6.

Hajimudin too has a medical disability. Fluid has collected in his brain and, as a result, he will need medical help soon or else he may suffer brain damage. Their father died of tuberculosis some seven years ago, and so for many years now they have been living on the streets. The family knows that but for Hunupa's days of begging, it would be hard to guess what might have become of them.

Manora, Hunupa's mother, has asthma and a medical condition that makes it very difficult for her to do any kind of manual labor, and so

In the streets of New Delhi, India, Hunupa Begum, 13, who has been blind for ten years, begs in order to help provide for her mother and younger brother.

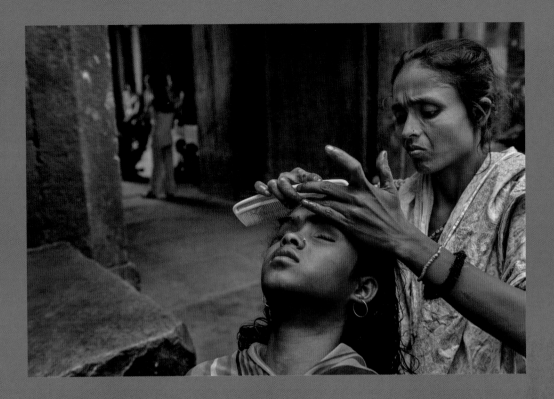

The Begum family all rely on Hunupa to provide for them. Nevertheless, in every way they can, they all care for each other. Hunupa's younger brother, Hajimudin Sheikh, 6, suffers from an abnormal level of fluid in his head and her mother, Manora Begum, 35, suffers from asthma as well as a growth in her womb. In spite of all of this, however, they remain a family.

Manora Begum and her family sleep in intense heat on the streets of New Delhi, and each night Manora fans her children to sleep outside of a mosque where she believes they will be safe.

her job is to be her children's caretaker. Hunupa begs twice a day. In the morning she begs long enough to collect the money to buy a late morning breakfast for her family, and later in the day she will beg again for several more hours until they have raised enough money to buy some food for dinner. When few have given, Hunupa resorts to asking local merchants for extra food. It is very hard to say no to her. This is the work that Hunupa does to support the family she loves.

They eat on the street beside the mosque and sleep on some tarps they spread out across the ground. In the evenings Hunupa's mother fans her two children until about 10 P.M. so that they might finally fall asleep and have enough energy to work again the next day. The heat in New Delhi can reach 125 degrees Fahrenheit during midsummer, and in the evening it may only cool down to 100. It is a wonder that they can sleep at all.

The life of Hunupa and her family is by no means rare. In fact, on any given day you can see thousands of children begging on the streets of New Delhi, and of course there are millions more around the world. All have their own stories, many suffer long days and many are exposed to the dangers of street work. At least Hunupa can be found under the watchful eye of her mother. ■

short list—a doctor, a soccer player, a teacher, or Nelson Mandela. They say this in spite of their simple rags and their distended stomachs and a life that doesn't seem like it will change anytime soon. Hopefully they will all survive another year, in spite of the summer's heat, the bulls that can gore them, malaria that can kill them, and the snakes and scorpions that are often far too close to where they may sit and rest for a moment. At the end of the day, they once again tie up the cows for the night with a rope their father weaved for them and go home to rest for yet another day of work tomorrow.

Top left: Older boys watch over their crops and land from the trees. Bottom left: The "cowboys" work hard to keep their cows off others' land to avoid confrontations. This is the life these boys lead instead of going to school.

Left: Alejandra, 39, and her son Enrique, 13, prepare skins made from the hides of the alpacas and llamas they watch over in the Akamani mountain range of Bolivia. Although done in a beautiful setting, right, this is very hard work, but it is work they must do in order to sell their leather at market and provide for their family.

IN THE MOUNTAINS OF BOLIVIA

At the opposite end of the world there are other children who go about this same task in a similar way, but instead of watching over cattle they care for sixty alpaca and llamas in the Akamani mountain range of Bolivia in an area called Caluyo, about an hour from the city of Qutapampa.

In this part of the world, the highlands of Bolivia, approximately 13,000 feet above sea level, residents live in homes with no insulation, no electricity, and no beds. Their water comes from streams that run off the snow-covered mountains. Their livelihood lies with their animals, for each animal produces about three pounds of fur each year, and each pound of fur is sold for 18 bolivianos, which amounts to about $2.50 U.S. All in all, this family may earn about $200 of income each year from the herd they watch over. Often, too, animals are skinned by the family's children for the leather is quite valuable and sold at market for clothing or to make saddles. This is a job often done by Enrique Kalancha Quispe (13) and his mother Alejandra (39). About three animals are killed annually to provide meat for the family, which is eaten with potatoes grown on their property. The herd's excrement is used for fuel to cook their food.

The children that live here start their day's work at 6 A.M., then go to school for several hours in the late morning and return in the midday to gather the

"With school, my father gone, and all the animals to care for, life is hard." — Alvaro Kalancha Quispe (9)

animals and place them in their pens for the evening. This work is usually done by 9-year-old Alvaro Kalancha Quispe.

At this altitude, there are no trees, so the children climb on rocks to count the animals in order to make sure that none have been lost. The school in and around this area of Bolivia only goes up to the eighth grade. Few children get beyond that level of education, for to do so would mean that they would have to leave their family and travel to the city of Charazani or La Paz.

The children of this family do much of the work associated with caring for their livestock without their father. He died some years ago, three days after he started experiencing some stomach pains. Although he was brought to the city of Qutapampa to get medical help, no one there could help him, and by the time the family had reached Bolivia's main hospital in La Paz the children's father had died. Although this was not the case in this family, people here often refuse to travel when they become ill and simply hope that they will get better. In many instances, that does not happen, and of course conditions worsen. This is true for many who live in remote areas of the world, and is true for the children who herd animals in the mountains of Bolivia.

Alvaro Kalancha Quispe, 9, opens the gate to the stone pen that holds the family's alpacas and llamas each morning so they can graze throughout the hillsides during the day. He then heads off to school, but must round them up again in the evening, for this is the work he does for his family.

Left: Aldahir and his mother were living on the streets before they were taken in and he was given a job as a pig farmer. Now they live together in a small shack with two beds. Aldahir, however, carries with him much sadness for he has missed much of his schooling and he is not sure where life will take him.

Right: Aldahir uses a motorbike to travel about the city looking for food to feed the pigs and his family.

has kindly given them a place to live, will eat the fresh food, but all the other waste must go to their pigs, which is boiled or cooked to kill the bacteria before it is fed to them.

This is all work that Aldahir must do each day in order to eventually get his pigs to market. The one saving grace that Aldahir has in his life is that recently he has found a little time to go to school. Though he is 13 years old, he is only in the second grade, for he has missed so many years of schooling that he is well behind other students of his age. Aldahir has few friends, if any, for between his work in the morning, walking to and from school, and coming home to clean pens and

feed the pigs, there is little time for anything else. Also, in the area in which he lives, there are no children, for it is not a place one would wish to live if one had children. His small shack has two beds, no appliances, no electricity, no running water, and no kitchen. The stove is simply an assortment of bricks, wood, and some pots. He now has a few books but wishes he had more.

Throughout the world, many of the world's poor raise pigs, for it is very cheap to feed pigs, they don't require much space, they produce large litters, and they remain quite a popular source of food, which can be easily sold at market. This is particularly true in Latin American countries. ∎

The Children of Bangladesh

MAKING THE CLOTHES WE WEAR

Her name is Sultana. She claims to be 14 years old and lives and works in the city of Dhaka, Bangladesh. Her day starts at around 6 A.M. when she wakes up and gets ready for her day. By 7 o'clock she leaves the small one-room shack where she lives with her mother and two younger siblings and walks an hour to work. Throughout the walk each morning, she dodges mud puddles, bicycle carts, cars, motorbikes, and other pedestrians. Just her walk to work and home again is a test of her agility and fate.

Sultana works in a garment factory where she is a stitcher's assistant, preparing zippers to be stitched into coats to be worn by children on the other side of the world. She has worked at this factory for a year. Each day she works from 8 A.M. to 8 P.M., walks home, and if she eats at all she has dinner at 10 at night, falls asleep, and does the same thing the next day. This is what she does at least six days a week. On every other Sunday she does get a day off, and on the remaining Sundays she works only until 5 P.M. Sultana seems never to smile, play, or have any kind of life of her own. In fact on most days you

Sultana, 14 (in blue wrap), lives in the city of Dhaka in Bangladesh, and works in a garment factory as a stitcher's assistant. She works twelve-hour days doing the same thing over and over again. She makes zippers for clothing that will be sold around the world. It is what she does to help her family.

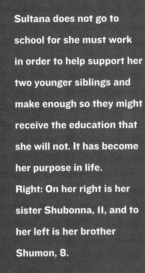

Sultana does not go to school for she must work in order to help support her two younger siblings and make enough so they might receive the education that she will not. It has become her purpose in life.
Right: On her right is her sister Shubonna, 11, and to her left is her brother Shumon, 8.

can find Sultana holding a zipper while staring aimlessly into space, as only an occasional breeze enters the factory in Dhaka's nearly 100-degree Fahrenheit heat. This kind of demeanor is common in young factory workers throughout the world who work at mindless tasks that force them to do the same thing over and over again.

Sultana had to leave school when she was in the fifth grade to help support her family. In this part of the world, when one or two children must leave school to help support a family, it is often the girls who are chosen for that task. Sultana's two siblings, Shumon and Shubonna, are 8 and 11 years old, respectively. In as much as she works, it is possible for them to stay in school. Sultana's mother is a laborer at a construction site in the city and removes rocks and dirt by hand. Although Sultana is happy to have a job and help her family, she and her mother make almost nothing. Sultana's father abandoned them years ago and so it is only Sultana and her mother who must now work to keep the family afloat.

Left: Sudeb, 13, works as a barber in his uncle's shop after dropping out of school. It is a trade he hopes to learn and possibly use to support himself in the future. For now, however, most of what he earns goes to his family.
Right: Sujon, 12, works as a shoe shine boy on a ferry boat on the Padma River. His family pulled him out of school to help earn money to pay for his sister's wedding.

THE BOY BARBER AND THE SHOESHINE BOY

At the landing near where the Nagorbai Ferry docks works Sudeb (13). He is a barber at his uncle's barbershop. Sudeb dropped out of school shortly after the third grade because his family needed him to learn a trade and earn some money. Ordinarily, a good barber may make 450 taka a day in Bangladesh, about $5.50 U.S. In Sudeb's case, however, what he earns over the course of a day goes to his family and he keeps only about 20 to 25 taka a day, or about 36 cents. It is pocket money and he uses it to buy his clothes, lunch, and candy.

Not far from where Sultana, Saiful, and Suded work, we find a shoeshine boy named Sujon (12). He works on the Nagorbai Ferry boat that runs back and forth from Nagorbai to Dowlodia every day. He works there with his father, who also shines shoes, and has been pulled out of school by his family and put to work in order to earn money to pay for his sister's upcoming marriage. He starts his day at about 4 A.M. and works from before sunrise to sunset. Over the course of the day, he crosses the Padma River twelve times and, during each crossing, tries to find travelers who are in need of a shoe shine. For every shoe shine, he gets 10 taka, or about 16 cents. When people are kind, they may sometimes give him 30 to 50 taka. For his day's work, he usually makes about 150 to 200 taka, or about $2.80, which he says is good money for a boy his age. Someday he hopes to make more, but for now this money belongs to his family.

This is the work that some children do in the country of Bangladesh. ∎

CHAPTER SEVEN

The Work of the Poor

As one continues to turn the pages of this book, it might be easy to come to the conclusion that the lives many of the world's poor lead are vastly different and those differences depend on where they live and what distinct challenges lie before them. Certainly, there is some truth to this, but as we have seen it is also true that the poor share many of the same problems, among them their struggles to live in safe and adequate housing, to acquire medical care, to receive an adequate education, to feed and care for their children, and to be given the respect and dignity due them as members of the human family. There exists, too, another defining aspect about the world's poor, and it is that together they often do work which many of us would prefer not to do, and in so doing take on many of the world's worst jobs. This chapter seeks to tell the story of such jobs as well as the people who take on these tasks.

Before getting started, however, let's address two quick questions and possibly disavow at least one myth. First, what are the kinds of conditions that are often found to exist among some of the world's worst jobs and, second, why do people take on such jobs? The conditions are many of the same kinds of working conditions that from time to time we have all heard about: long working hours, little pay,

Throughout the world, the poor are often asked to take on some of our worst jobs. Here, a young man in Ghana, West Africa, burns and sifts through discarded computers in hopes of finding any valuable metals that may have been left behind, a process that, if lucky, brings him a dollar a day.

exploit and with this exploitation so goes the lives of some of the world's poorest children.

Manual Scavenging in India

Throughout India modern toilets are still somewhat difficult to come by and when one feels the need to relieve him/herself, one does so either in fields, in a nearby riverbed, or in a public toilet of one kind or another. Few have modern toilets at home, particularly in many of the rural areas of the country, and those who do often live in large cities where sewage systems have long been in need of repair, if they work at all. For this reason, India employs sewage workers or "manual scavengers," about one million such workers in all. They work both in cities and in rural areas of the country, and four out of five are women.

This job, probably the worst of the worst jobs in the world, is not coincidentally done by some of the poorest and most marginalized people on earth, 95 percent of whom are Dalits. In India, largely because the poor have few options in life and because it is a job that must be done by someone, many believe it should be done by those who have been born into the lowest caste in society, namely Dalits (or the "untouchables"), those on India's bottom rung of the caste system hierarchy. This is a system that was, in theory, constitutionally abolished in India over sixty years ago, but of course in reality it still works its way into the everyday lives of millions upon millions of Indians, many of whom do not only partake in this occupation but are often forced to work as street sweepers, tannery workers, brick kiln workers, rag pickers, beggars, and those who are assigned the job of disposing of dead bodies of the poor often found on the street.

There are at least three ways in which "manual scavenging," or *maila dhona* (lifting feces), occurs. First, and when done by women in many of India's rural areas, human feces are swept manually from some nine million public, as well as private, dry latrines throughout thousands of villages. These dry latrines are concrete enclosed rooms where people enter, place their feet upon raised concrete steps, squat, and defecate on the concrete floor.

The only equipment the women who sweep these floors have is a broom and tin plate, which they use to scoop up the human feces from the cement floor. The waste is then placed in baskets and carried by women on their shoulders or head to designated disposal areas in and around a village. From there it is carried off by truck to a dump site. It has been said that the worst time to do this kind of work is during the raining season, for when the rain comes the feces get wet and seep through the baskets into the women's hair, face, and clothing. When this occurs, women must learn to live with the smell and often it is hard to eat their dinners in the evening. For this, women receive approximately 42 rupees a day, or about 91 cents U.S. Sometimes, however, municipalities pay workers very late, if at all, for their work. This is constantly a problem and causes great hardship. Also, when the dry latrine belongs to a private individual or family, they sometimes decide to pay these workers only with some leftover food rather than rupees. As a result, some days these workers come home with no money at all.

A second manner in which this work is done involves men. Here, men go down into latrine pits or septic tanks and, in doing so, immerse themselves in human waste. They often do this with no protective gear and use a bucket to gather solids from the bottom of the pit. As a result of their continuous exposure to human waste, however, these men suffer from a number of ailments. Among them are respiratory infections, gastrointestinal disorders, and trachoma (a form of bacterial conjunctivitis that can result in blindness). On occasion male workers who are lowered into these latrine pits have died as a result of carbon monoxide poisoning and, when coupled with their overall poor health, they are, as a group, far more at risk of dysentery, malaria, and typhoid.

Because of the manner in which people were being used to do this kind of work, in 1993 the Indian Parliament enacted the Employment of Manual Scavengers and Construction of

Text continues on page 226

Asif, 13, was abandoned years ago. He lives and sleeps in train stations in the city of New Delhi, India, and jumps on moving train cars from station to station, stopping to collect recyclables or other valuables to then sell. It is the only job he has ever had.

Sonu Bahot:
A Day in His Life

Sonu Bahot (36) starts his day at 4 o'clock each and every morning. He travels three hours by train and bus to get to a job that requires him to strip down to his underwear and submerge his body into a swirl of decaying human excrement and various other kinds of sediment that one might find in the 3,700 miles of sewer pipes beneath the city streets of New Delhi, India. He is a New Delhi sewage worker, sometimes called *safai karmacharis,* or cleaning workers, a job he has had for over sixteen years, and a job that when combined with the amount of time he travels to and from work takes his entire day, arriving home about 9 P.M. to have dinner with his wife and three children, sleep a little, and get up the next day to do it all again.

The sewers that Sonu enters, which in most cases are hundreds of years old, require that he go into a manhole about 7 feet in depth, look and feel around for the material that is clogging the pipes, gather it with a small flat shovel, place it into a bucket, and pull the bucket up from the hole to his waiting coworkers, who then dump out the black sludge on the street. To do this, he also uses a steel bar to loosen the sewage and gather it up with his hands. These sewer pipes were never intended to accommodate the amount of waste produced in a city the size of New Delhi, and because the city cannot afford to rebuild its ever aging infrastructure men are used as tools to clean out and fix pipes that no longer work.

The truth is that the use of human beings in this manner has never been found to be particularly unreasonable by most in and around New Delhi because it is work that has been done for ages by those in India who are considered "untouchables." Sonu is one such "untouchable," a member of a subcaste within the Dalit community called Valmikis. Many Dalits in India are thought suitable by the Hindu religion to do some of the most horrendous and unclean jobs the country has to offer, and because of their status in life they are physically shunned by all who subscribe to this way of thinking. The Valmikis do this work because they have few options in life, are desperately poor, are discriminated against in a variety of settings, and most people in India have little pity for them. It is a caste system that, although illegal, remains a big part of the cultural beliefs and traditions of many of India's people.

Sonu, not too long ago, purchased for himself a plastic helmet. It is the only piece of safety equipment he owns. The company he works for

Sonu Bahot, 36, works to unclog old sewage pipes of decaying human feces, which clings to his body. He does so by climbing down manholes with little more than a plastic helmet and his underwear. It is a job relegated to India's "untouchables."

materials found inside. These gases can prove deadly to workers. In fact, about 200 such workers die each year in the city of Delhi from asphyxiation after too much gas has entered their lungs. Also, when disturbing these sites, cockroaches and rats scatter about and often jump on the workers. This is not a pleasant site.

Nevertheless, after sixteen years of service, Sonu is paid the equivalent of only $2.90 U.S. a day for his work, and with that he supports a family of five and somehow brings home enough money to keep his three children in school. Mr. Bahot says he has no future, but it is work he must do for the sake of his children. He believes nothing will change anytime soon but at some point he will have to retire, because of either illness or the fact that his company hired someone else who might be willing to do his work for less. He, of course, has no retirement or health plan and hopes only that his children will finish school before he becomes too ill to work or dies. Every day he suffers from rashes all over his body and often his eyes become infected with one type of bacteria or another. He knows too that some of his 8,000 coworkers who work throughout the city of New Delhi have died from tuberculosis and/or hepatitis caused by the work they do.

At the end of Mr. Bahot's workday he gets some help out of this city sewer from a coworker while the stench associated with his job remains evident in the faces of passersby who cover their noses with their saris while Sonu proceeds to wash off much of the muck that has adhered to his body. It is the work of the "untouchables." To an outsider, this seems to be a life without dignity, yet it is a life so many in India lead. ∎

Above: As Sonu emerges from a New Delhi sewer, passersby often cover their noses from the stench and fumes that can be overwhelming. Far right: With the help of a coworker, Sonu rinses off and hopes to avoid infections that can sometimes prove to be fatal.

does not provide him protective clothing, gloves, or even a protective mask or glasses to keep material away from places on his body that may be prone to infection. He finds the helmet useful because if he cuts his head on a pipe or rock it would almost immediately become infected. Also, if he hits his head on a hard surface he could slip into unconsciousness and drown in excreta. Many sewer workers have drowned while working in these pipes.

The day these photographs were taken, the temperature on this busy street in the heart of New Delhi was 107 degrees Fahrenheit. When these sewers are opened under these conditions noxious fumes are released because of the decomposing

The Dalai Lama's ski trip

Editor's note: The Dalai Lama visited the United States this month, meeting with President Barack Obama and saying a prayer to open a session of the Senate. But a generation ago it was quite a different trip when he came to the States as a recent Nobel laureate.

BY DOUGLAS PRESTON

In the mid '80s, I was living in Santa Fe, N.M., making a shabby living writing magazine articles, when a peculiar assignment came my way. I had become friendly with a group of Tibetan exiles who lived in a compound where they ran a business selling Tibetan rugs, jewelry and religious items.

The Dalai Lama, who had received the Nobel Peace Prize in 1989, accepted an invitation to visit Santa Fe during a tour of the United States and said he would be happy to come for a week. At the time, he wasn't the international celebrity he is today. He traveled with only a half-dozen monks, most of whom spoke no English. He had no handlers, advance men, interpreters, press people or travel coordinators.

Nor did he have any money. So James Rutherford, who ran the gov-

Photo courtesy of Bob Shaw

In 1991, the Dalai Lama was amazed to see skiing for the first time; soon after, a waitress asked the question no one else had dared to.

ernor's art gallery in the state capitol building and had a rare gift for organization, undertook to arrange the Dalai Lama's visit.

Rutherford began making phone calls. He borrowed a stretch limousine from a wealthy art dealer, and he asked his brother, Rusty, to drive it. He persuaded the proprietors of Rancho Encantado, a luxury resort outside Santa Fe, to provide the Dalai Lama and his monks with free food and lodging. He called the state police and arranged for a security detail.

Among the many phone calls Rutherford made, one was to me. The Dalai Lama, he explained, was a person who would stop and talk to anyone who asked him a question. He treated all people the same, from the president of the United States to a bum on the street, giv-

See DALAI LAMA, 4P

Fati and Those Who Live On an E-Waste Dumpsite

Her name is Fati. She is 8 years old and she lives in a place called Agbogbloshie, Accra, the capital city of Ghana in West Africa. Fati works at what she does because she has almost no other options. Brought to this area of the city by her mother some years ago from a village in northern Ghana, Fati now finds herself in a prison of poison, wishing she could return home. Her mother left her village with only her, while Fati's three brothers remained at home with their father. He had four other wives and had no further use for Fati's mother who now works at a nearby market as a porter carrying the food of others to their respective homes (see chapter 5, profile one).

Fati works with other children throughout the day and sees her mother when she returns to their home, which consists of a 10 x 10–foot, one-room shack they share with other women and girls. It is where they sleep each night and rise early each morning to put in yet another day's work. The bucket Fati balances on her head is what she uses to collect items from the garbage of the rich, for she works in what has been called an e-waste dumpsite and spends each day sorting through materials that have traveled to her front yard from some of the world's wealthiest nations. The tears on her face are caused by the pain

In an e-waste dump that kills nearly everything that it touches, Fati, 8, works with other children searching through hazardous waste in hopes of finding whatever she can to exchange for pennies in order to survive. While balancing a bucket on her head with the little metal she has found, tears stream down her face as the result of the pain that comes with the malaria she contracted some years ago. This is her life.

that she endures each day as a result of the malaria she contracted about a year ago as well as the simple state of her life and her hope for something more.

E-waste, or electronic waste, is made up of old televisions, printers, cameras, DVD players, music speakers, computers, laptops, phones, MP3 players, PDAs, and all of those modern gadgets that many in the Western world give each other as gifts each year or buy for themselves and can seemingly no longer do without. These are largely the toys and tools of the West and are used in technologically advanced countries where today they are produced at an astonishing rate. In fact, each year worldwide, nearly 50 million metric tons of electronic material is produced. Much of this is used to replace items that have gotten too old to be of any practical use or are no longer as sleek as some of the newer devices that have hit markets worldwide.

The problem, of course, is that electronic waste is by no means benign. It is, in fact, hazardous and contains many toxic substances. Tragic but true, as with much of the world's waste, many rich countries export these waste materials to poor or developing countries, most often China, Vietnam, India, Pakistan, Nigeria, and Ghana, and it is the poor of those countries who often dismantle these products in an effort to reap whatever valuable metals they can harvest, or in some cases try to sell these products to brokers or at a market for whatever they can get.

The city of Guiyu, China, is probably ground zero for the massive global dumping of e-waste. There, some 150,000 workers, mostly women, search through tons of material each day and in doing so either burn off plastics or use acid to collect valuable metals from the e-waste and take what they find to recyclers in order to eke out something of a living for themselves. Guiyu has become one of the most polluted cities in the world. The pollution comes from the lead, cadmium, mercury, and beryllium as well as burning the brominated flame retardants that are used in the circuit boards and in the plastics that house the equipment. As a result of the environmental degradation that occurs in this city, the water is no longer drinkable and residents there suffer from brain damage, burning in their lungs, skin rashes, headaches, vertigo, ulcers, and birth defects at rates far higher than in surrounding areas. Moreover, nearly all their children suffer from lead poisoning as a result of the extraordinarily high levels of lead in the soil and groundwater. All this suffering can be traced to the hundred or so truckloads of electronic waste that arrive there every day.

In Ghana, where Fati lives, it is mostly poor and abandoned migrant children who work in this graveyard of electronic waste on what used to be pristine land on the edge of the Korle Lagoon just west of Accra's central business district. They do so with few or no tools. They walk through charred earth with little more than rubber flip-flops on their feet while all around them people are burning off plastic to try to get to the metals found inside the waste. What they look for is copper, brass, aluminum, zinc, silver, and gold, which they resell to buy food. Using nothing but their hands, and sometimes a magnet, they will search for days in order to find something of value. Throughout the dump, you will find products by manufacturers such

Far left: What used to be the pristine waters of the Korle Lagoon in the city of Accra, Ghana, West Africa, is now an electronics dumpsite. Above: Here children work all day to collect whatever scraps they can, then try to wash the carbon soot off their feet that has attached itself to their young bodies.

The boys that work on this e-waste dumpsite burn computers in order to extract any valuable metals that might fall to the ground. In the process they expose themselves to toxic fumes that gather in their clothes, skin, and lungs. These cast-off computers from the Western world are shipped to Ghana, West Africa.

Above: Philimon, 14, is homeless and works in this polluted world for it is all he has in life.
Far right: Ayisha, 10, has experienced the same fate. They are impoverished children that few seem to care about and have been left here with few options in life.

third grade after his father could no longer care for him. Most nights he sleeps on the street and when it rains he sleeps under someone's awning or in a truck. Recently he was brought to a hospital in need of medical attention after suffering heat stroke while working in the sun at the Agbogbloshie dump. Other street children tried to help pay his medical bills but few had any money. Eventually he was released only to go back to work in the dump.

On some days, Philimon finds nothing of value and makes no money. On a good day he may make as much as 2 Ghana cedi or about $1.28 U.S. This is not much of a reward considering the toxins that not only seep into his skin but surely must also find their way into his lungs. Moreover, not only does this work affect these children and workers in the dump, but because it creates immense damage to the air this affects those who happen to live in this part of Accra. As evidence of what has occurred here, the Korle lagoon is now a dead body of water, and nothing can live there, not even worms.

Not far from where Philimon works sits Ayisha (10). Girls and boys work these dumps separately and sleep in separate shacks located on the dump site. Each night Ayisha sleeps with ten female children in a tiny room where they gather to try to protect themselves from those who may wish to harm them or abduct them in the night. This occurs with some frequency in Agbogbloshie. They are all squatters who pay rent to the person who built their shack but have almost no property of their own. Ayisha is one of Fati's friends and sometimes helps watch over her while Fati's mother is working. Ayisha also is quite sad about how her life has turned out. She is an orphan and often feels she must simply

as Philips, Canon, Dell, Microsoft, Nokia, Siemens, Sony, and Apple. When these materials are burned off, a thick black blanket of smoke is created and fills the air, and the chemicals that are burned off make the environment a kind of hell on earth for the air that these impoverished workers and children breathe is toxic.

Carbon residue and soot also form on the skin of those who work here, making their hands and faces charcoal black. As evidence of this, one can examine Philimon's hands. He is 14 years old and he uses his hands to sift through the burned-over soil to find bits of precious metals. He is homeless and was forced to leave school when he was in the

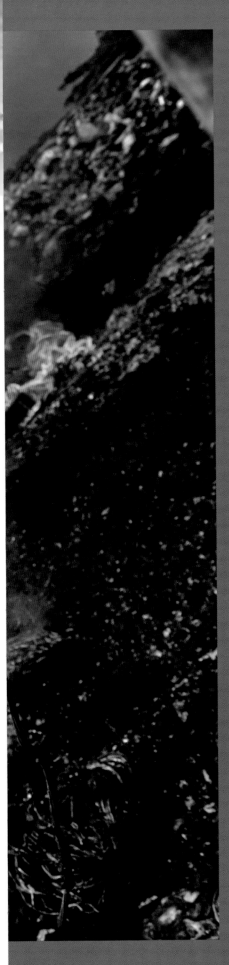

Older boys, such as Mohamed Abukari, 17 (framed center), usually are first to burn and pick through the residue of discarded computers for copper wiring or any other valuable metals. In the background, other boys are getting ready to ignite more items into flames. These boys make the most money at this site while younger children, who go through what's left, make almost nothing.

take a break from her workday to sit on her bucket and ponder her life. Surrounded by burning waste, it is no wonder that on some days she cannot work at all.

Mohamed Abukari (17) has worked in the Agbogbloshie dump for some years. He has no education and each night sleeps on the floor of a tiny wood structure that surrounds this dumpsite. For his sleeping quarters, he is charged one Ghana cedi a day (about 64 cents). Each day he must earn more than that simply to survive. Mohamed is often one of the first each morning to decide what must be burned and possibly the first to look through recently burned materials to find what might be salvaged. Because he is so often near toxic smoke, his skin and clothes are blackened by soot and, as with many who live and work here, he often coughs up black phlegm. As one of the first to retrieve metals from the burned e-waste, Mohamed can sometimes make as much as 8 Ghana cedi a day, about $5.00 U.S. Nevertheless, on some days, much like others, he makes nothing at all. On those days he must go into whatever he has saved from a previous day to eat and pay his rent. With no skills, no education, no friends of any influence, and little ability to purchase clean or presentable clothing, he is not sure what else life might hold for him. Until something changes he will continue to search through what he has burned.

Probably more than any other country on earth, the United States is most responsible for what these children and workers endure, since of all the countries in the world that export electronic waste the United States exports the most. Ironically,

almost half of the states in the United States have banned the dumping of hazardous electronic waste within their own borders. In those states these materials must be either dismantled and cleaned legally before they are disposed of or disposed of in another state or outside the country. Unfortunately, it is nearly always cheaper to just send those products elsewhere than to clean them properly, and in most cases that is exactly what is done. This is possible because the United States is one of only a very few countries that has not ratified (or agreed to) the one international law that makes the dumping of electronic waste by rich countries into poor countries illegal. That law is called the Basel Convention on the Control of Transboundary Movements of Hazardous Wastes and Their Disposal. This convention (or treaty) was first adopted in March of 1989 but became law in May of 1992. Again and unfortunately, of the 179 countries that have agreed to the provisions of this treaty, the United States is not one of them and so it is not bound by its provisions.

Sadly, too, is the fact that it is because many states forbid the disposal of the e-waste in their own landfills that we "recycle" it. Unfortunately what "recycle" means in practice in this instance is that we simply ship our waste to another country and call it "recycling," leaving it up to others to deal with the consequences of the disposal of hazardous waste. In more cases than we would like to admit, it is the world's poor, as well as their children, who suffer because no one wishes to pay the price of disposing of these products in a safe and sane way. This is another example of a job the poor will do to survive and another way in which poverty kills. ■

Surviving on the Waste of Others

On any given day and in nearly any country around the world thousands, if not millions, of men, women, and children survive by collecting, sorting, and selling the waste of others. It is a job of last resort and a job taken up by those who often have few options in life, because of either the discrimination they have faced, their lack of education, their lack of a system of support, or simply because it is the only job that they have ever done. Recycling, at least when done by people in the streets, has been called a job of last resort because it requires no employer, no hiring process, and there is no shortage of waste. In fact, in nearly all of the major cities of the world, the production of waste has greatly outpaced the ability of cities to clean up what they have produced. Formal or commercial systems of collection and sanitation are often way behind what many growing cities have come to require and, in a city such as Lima, Peru, 20 percent of all its waste is gathered up by impoverished people working on the streets. More and more developing countries are only now beginning to come up with an effective means of collecting and disposing of waste and have come to realize that, in many cases, there is money to be

Erika Gonzales, 36, forms a trainlike procession as she walks with three of her children as well as her grandchild fastened to her back through the streets of Lima, Peru, collecting recyclables. In Lima, 20 percent of all its waste is gathered up in this manner.

Above: Mrs. Gonzales's children do not go to school. They are too poor and she needs their help to gather up what they find.

Far right: At day's end, they turn in items they have collected to the local recycling center and hope that they have raised enough money to pay their next day's rent.

had in recyclables, and for environmental reasons it is far better to recycle items than to pour them into just another landfill. This has created many jobs for those in need of work. One such person is Erika Orihuela Gonzales.

Erika Gonzales, although only 36, has six children, four of whom live with her along with her grandson, Dayron. They live in a single room in a district of Lima, Peru, called Villa El Salvador. At present, they are two months behind in their rent and, as a result, will likely be evicted soon. This will not be unusual since the family seldom has enough money to pay rent and is often in need of help from others. Mrs. Gonzales's livelihood, along with that

of her family, depends on the waste of others. She works as a "waste picker." She starts working every day by 8 A.M. trying to find and collect recyclable items with her children. She pushes a cart around the city to help transport her children as well as the items they happen to collect. The children help her search for different recyclables: paper, plastic, glass, and metals. The materials are then taken to a recycling center where Mrs. Gonzales sells what they have collected. On a good day she can make about 6 to 12 soles or about $2 to $4 U.S. This is hardly enough to feed her family and provides her with no additional money for rent, medical care, or schooling. Her children work with her throughout the day. She tries to get the children home before 8 P.M. because they are tired and need to eat. Dinner is sometimes prepared for them by Mrs. Gonzales's sister, who lives nearby, since Mrs. Gonzales herself has no kitchen. After the children are fed, Mrs. Gonzales goes out again until about 11 P.M. to find what she can so she doesn't have to start the next day with nothing in her cart.

Her children do not attend school. There is simply no money, and Mrs. Gonzales needs their help to find and collect whatever they can to sell. Her children from a second husband, Naisha, Anderson, and Nicoll, range in age from 2 to 6. They often scramble about and collect what they can while Mrs. Gonzales carries Dayron (8 months) on her back. Mrs. Gonzalez has three other children, ages 16, 14 and 10. Her 16-year-old daughter, Josselin, the mother of her grandson, Dayron, is at home for the day. Dayron's father left before he was born. Mrs. Gonzales's two other children, both boys, live with their father and work in the agricultural

fields in the countryside of Peru. She has not seen them for years after having to run away from her very abusive husband. Unfortunately, her second husband has treated her in much the same way and not only beat her but also forcefully kept her from using birth control, and so today this is what she must do to support what is left of her family.

Many say that the work waste pickers do in Lima, as well as throughout the world, is good for cities, the environment, and the poor. Many insist this is true in spite of studies that reveal many of the negative health consequences associated with this type of work. These consequences have a disproportionate impact on the poor and include chronic bronchitis, asthma, and anemia, which are mostly the results of exposure to chemicals, metals, smoke, and dust. These conditions affect children hardest and, when coupled with malnutrition, leave them at grave risk. Dayron, for example, is asthmatic and has to use an inhaler as well as go to the doctor when it becomes difficult for him to breath. The cause of his asthma is uncertain, but when he is sick the family goes without food so that they can pay for treating the baby. When money is short Mrs. Gonzales will also add water to chicken broth for the family to eat and try to stretch what little they have and still feed her family. They live on the edge and have been dealt few options in life. They have been left to survive on the waste of others. It is a story that remains true for so many all over the world. ■

At bedtime, Mrs. Gonzales nurses her youngest child Naisha, 2, while her oldest daughter Josselin, 16, in the background, does the same for her child, Dayron, 8 months. In total, this family of six live day to day on two to four dollars per day, in addition to what Josselin might earn, if and when she can find work.

exploitive and, at worst, demeaning, dehumanizing, and/or dangerous to their health and safety? The answer is complex, uneven, and ever changing.

The good news is that yes, laws do exist; however, these laws must always be brought into play with the ever changing realities of the world's condition in mind, as well as the disparities that continue to exist worldwide as to what might be appropriate or inappropriate or even necessary with regard to working conditions that people experience in light of a particular nation's level of development and its historical, cultural, and religious traditions. One would be quite naive to think that the millions upon millions of the world's poor who take many of the jobs that no one would do given a choice have much in the way of power to demand that things change for the better. They most often take these jobs out of desperation, out of a need to survive or feed their families, and in the hope that even if life may not change for them it might improve for their children.

The single most important organization in the world responsible for the fair treatment of workers worldwide is the International Labor Organization (ILO). Established in 1919 as an arm of the League of Nations and later a specialized agency of the United Nations, the ILO has the very difficult job of attempting to get otherwise sovereign and independent nations to agree to abide by a standard of appropriate behavior when making use of human labor worldwide. Again, in light of the diversity of opinions that exist as to the appropriateness of labor conditions and the use of human capital, getting countries to agree on a minimum standard of care that should be offered to all workers worldwide has been very difficult indeed. Nevertheless, over its nearly hundred-year history some of the world's most important labor concerns have been addressed and the ILO has been able to acquire the ratification of many international conventions (or treaties) that seek to improve the conditions of workers and labor in general worldwide. Some of their most important work is embodied in the following treaties.

- **The Forced Labor Convention, 1930:** requires the suppression of forced or compulsory labor in all its forms with certain exceptions, such as when applied to military service, or when applied to convict labor properly supervised, or in emergencies, such as wars, fires, earthquakes, etc.
- **The Freedom of Association and Protection of the Right to Organize Convention, 1948:** establishes the right of all workers and employers to form and join organizations of their own choosing without prior authorization and lays down a series of guarantees for the free functioning of such organizations without interference by public authorities.
- **The Right to Organize and Collective Bargaining Convention, 1949:** provides for protection against anti-union discrimination, for protection of workers' and employers' organizations against acts of interference from each other, and for measures to promote collective bargaining.
- **The Equal Remuneration Convention, 1951:** calls for equal pay for men and women for work of equal value.
- **The Abolition of Forced Labor Convention, 1957:** prohibits the use of any form of forced or compulsory labor as a means of political coercion or education, punishment for the expression of political or ideological views, workforce mobilization, labor discipline, punishment for participation in strikes, or discrimination.
- **The Discrimination (Employment and Occupation) Convention, 1958:** calls for a national policy to eliminate discrimination in access to employment, training and working conditions, on grounds of race, color, sex, religion, political opinion, national extraction, or social origin in order to promote equality in opportunity and treatment.
- **The Minimum Age Convention, 1973:** aims at the abolition of child labor, stipulating that the minimum age for admission to employment shall not be less than the age of completion of compulsory schooling, and in any case not less than 15 years (14 for developing countries).

Moreover, in the early 1990s the ILO issued additional directives concerning the need for more oversight of worldwide working conditions. Of concern at that time were the implementation of measures to improve the safety and health of pregnant workers, women workers who had recently given birth, and women who were breastfeeding. Of specific concern were the tasks such women workers were asked to perform, the number of hours they were required to work, and whether a right to maternity leave existed. Also, during this time, a directive was issued that sought to better protect young workers and asked the agreeing members of the ILO to take necessary measures to prohibit the employment of children (under the age of 15), and ensure that the employment of adolescents (between the ages of 15 and 18) was strictly controlled under the conditions provided for in the law. These regulations addressed the types of employment youth could be asked to perform as well as issues regarding working hours, night work, rest periods, and annual leave.

When attempting to enforce these provisions of international law and agreements as to the treatment of laborers worldwide, the ILO makes use of a number of strategies to encourage member nations and/or multinational corporations to abide by the laws and/or the agreements they have entered into. These strategies might include the public admonishment of their conduct, fines of one kind or another, and/or the termination of some of the privileges associated with being a member of the ILO. Unfortunately, sometimes these laws do not cover the particular

harm involved or the country or corporation perpetrating the harm. Sometimes, too, as we have seen throughout this chapter, in some countries you will find little in the way of public outcry to change that which exists even when it is clear to most that much harm is being done, and in these circumstances the practice and work that the poor often must do continues.

Fortunately, over the course of human history, things have changed for the better. No longer is slave labor used in the same manner or in the numbers that we have witnessed in the past and no longer can it be said that workers have no rights, whether they be young, old, man, woman, or disabled. Nevertheless, there is much work to do to continue to ensure that all workers regardless of their status and condition in life be treated with human dignity.

Note: While the United Nations does not deal with labor matters as such, and recognizes the ILO as the specialized agency responsible for taking appropriate action in this area of law, some United Nations instruments do cover matters of labor, the most important of which are the International Covenant on Economic, Social and Cultural Rights and the International Covenant on Civil and Political Rights, which are legally binding human rights agreements. Both of these covenants were adopted in 1966 and became law ten years later. Also extremely important in this area of law are the Convention on the Elimination of All Forms of Racial Discrimination, the Elimination of all Forms of Discrimination against Women, and the International Convention on the Rights of the Child. ∎

CHAPTER EIGHT

Women at Work

"Women do two-thirds of the world's work, receive ten percent of the world's income, and own one percent of the means of production."
Richard Robbins, Professor of Anthropology
State University of New York

This statement was made well over a decade ago and is often quoted by those who wish to point out the vast differences between men and women with regard to work and economic power in our world. Unfortunately, although this statement was made some years ago, it remains as true today as when it was first expressed. This chapter will largely address some of these differences as well as some of the ways women endeavor to make ends meet worldwide. This chapter should be distinguished from chapter 5 where we addressed how women around the world, in spite of how often they are so poorly treated, do so much to keep families together, rear their children, and often provide for the additional support needed to give their children a chance at a better life. In doing so, we presented information about how women are discriminated against, even before they are born, how they are the first to be forced to drop out of school in order to help their mothers at home, how they often work long hours at sometimes demeaning jobs, or worse, are sold into marriages at a young age, or have to provide dowries to their husbands in

Believe it or not, many women throughout the world work as manual laborers on construction sites, sometimes with few or no men to help them. This is particularly true in countries such as India where women every day leave their humble homes to go off and try to make a dollar a day.

order to marry, and even when married are far too often abandoned or abused by those who have only recently entered their lives. Women suffer through all this only to grow old and raise a second generation of children in countries that provide them with little in the way of support and/or rights in their later years.

In this chapter we will instead concentrate on the work that some of the world's poorest women do around the world. This is work they often do simply to survive and provide for their children. When reading this chapter, it is important to remember several things. First, please know that it would be a mistake to read this chapter without reflecting back on chapter 2, and the fact that most of the world's poor women are subsistence farmers and that women grow most of the world's crops. This is particularly true in sub-Saharan Africa as well as the Caribbean. Women do far more than their share to feed the world, and while doing so they are traditionally the world's homemakers, servants, seamstresses, teachers, childcare providers, house cleaners, sweepers, cooks, and all-around service providers. Yes, women perform all of these occupations, often for little remuneration, and sometimes for even less thanks.

Second, and with regard to work in general, it can easily be said that there are three kinds of work that poor women do. Some women, for example, participate in what is called the "formal labor market." This means they often have an employer, they may get paid regularly, they often work alongside men and often have specific tasks, hours, and responsibilities within a prescribed job description. The work is often regulated, and laws may exist to protect workers' safety and rights. It should be noted, however, that poor women do not participate in the formal labor market to the extent that men do. This is largely due to the discrimination faced by women as well as their generally lower levels of education and perceived inability to handle "man's work." Also women are generally in far greater need of flexibility regarding working hours in as much as they are nearly always responsible for the

EARNINGS OF WOMEN VS. MEN WORLDWIDE

Regions of the World	Average Earnings of Women per/year	Average Earnings of Men per/year	Percentage of Men's Earnings
Industrialized nations	$21,000	$37,000	57%
Latin America / Caribbean	$4,000	$10,000	40%
East Asia / Pacific	$4,000	$6,500	62%
Middle East / North Africa	$2,000	$7,000	28%
South Asia	$1,000	$2,500	39%
Sub-Saharan Africa	$1,000	$2,000	51%

Note: Estimated earnings are defined as gross domestic product per capita as measured in U.S. dollars at 2003 prices adjusted as appropriate. Source UNICEF (2007).

care of their children, for the upkeep of their households, and for a myriad of other tasks that many poor women must do simply because they are women in a world governed by men. Even when women do manage to work side by side with men, they still get paid far less than what men earn for the same work. This is true in nearly all countries.

Women also work in the "informal labor market." In fact, in the developing world, it is how most women bring home some income. A term first coined in 1972, the informal labor market includes jobs individuals create largely for themselves, such as farming, fishing, house cleaning, or the sale of one's goods and services at a market. Here there are generally no specific employers or companies for whom to work. Few regulations govern the way one earns her money and much is controlled by the weather, crop yields, time of year, the economic conditions within a certain community, village, or city, and many other factors that may been estimated that women spend twice as much time doing unpaid work than men do. This work is often grueling, but because many believe that "work" should not be considered "work" unless it is paid, little recognition is ever given to the unpaid work that women do in spite of this great contribution on the part of working women worldwide. The truth is, but for that which women provide to our children, families, and extended families, life as we know it would be very different indeed. Unfortunately, it is because women must often put so much of their time into unpaid work that they have substantially less time to work in either the formal or informal labor markets and economies. This keeps them in poverty and often makes them economically dependent on men, leaving them at a disadvantage and making it harder for them to better their lives. Add to this the fact that in some countries women cannot own or inherit property and have a great deal of difficulty acquiring credit and it is no wonder that they, along with their children, continue to remain the poorest of the poor. (See chapter 5.)

Another kind of work and/or problem that the poor of the world are exposed to is work they are far too often "trafficked" into or, to be clear, work that many say amounts to the modern equivalent of slavery. It is a practice that is illegal, at least in most of the world, and can be identified by examining three key elements associated with the act of human trafficking. First is the fact that this conduct usually involves the recruiting, transporting, transferring, harboring, and receiving of a person. Second, it is accomplished through the use of force, coercion, fraud, deception, or the outright purchase of a human being from someone having power, control, or custody over that person. And third, the transfer is made for the purpose of exploitation.

The law that applies to this kind of conduct is called the Protocol to Prevent, Suppress and Punish Trafficking in Persons (especially women and children). It was adopted by the UN in 2000 and became law in December of 2003 as part of

be outside one's control. Sometimes the work is piecemeal and done part-time on top of other work. Often, too, the poor are quite resourceful in creating these jobs. For example, a woman may take in the laundry of others, make baskets or crafts for sale, take in sewing jobs in the evenings to make a few extra coins, or sweep the storefronts of several local established businesses. When men enter this market they often create their own jobs and may become rickshaw drivers, porters, shoe shiners, street dentists, butchers, barbers, and even earwax removers. Because of the situation that many women find themselves in around the world, they often turn to the informal labor market in order to simply survive. This is true because the hours one might work are often flexible, sometimes minimal skills are needed, and most of these jobs require little investment.

Finally, we all should realize that women spend much of their lives working at jobs that do not pay anything at all. In fact, it has

Text continues on page 258

On a hillside overlooking the city of Huaycan, Peru, sit three boys who await their mother's return home. Their mother sings on the street and in buses to try to make a living and provide for them, yet not even the 10 x 10–foot home they live in is theirs. At least they have each other.

A Bus Singer in Huaycan, Peru

At the end of a long day, on a hillside overlooking the city of Huaycan, Peru, sit three of Maria Guzman's four sons, Diego (18), Jefferson (6), and Ronaldino (10), outside their 10 x 10–foot shack where their family of six sleeps each night. It is a home with no bathroom, only one broken bed, and nothing but an open fire over which to cook. The home they live in does not belong to them. It is a makeshift shelter constructed illegally on this hillside from which the local authorities are trying to evict them.

To support her children, Maria Guzman (41) has created her own job in what has been called the informal labor market or economy. She is what they call a "bus singer." In order to gather up the few dollars she needs to survive, she simply boards a bus, sings about her life, and hopes that those on the bus will be touched by her songs, her life, and the needs of her children enough to offer her some spare change and some hope, at least to get through another day. The advantage of boarding a bus is that for at least a short time Maria has a captive audience and an opportunity to move enough of the individuals on the bus to make

her stay on the bus worthwhile. Those who ride the bus in this area of Peru are by no means well off, so at best she will receive only a few pennies on any given ride and most of the time nothing at all, particularly if the patrons on the bus have given to her before.

Maria also sings in the marketplace, often accompanied by her children, who join her after school to sell candies alongside their mother in hopes that they will make a little extra money to buy something to eat. Maria has no employer, no job description, no schedule per se, but she knows that she needs to make a certain amount of money each day just to survive. Often this requires her to work until 9 o'clock in the evening.

One of Maria's problems is that her choices in life have been limited because of the men she has encountered. A survivor of domestic violence, she carries many of the scars of abuse throughout her body. In some cases these scars have disfigured her, and for this reason alone it has been difficult for her to find a more traditional job or work in a retail establishment. She has been reduced to singing on the bus and the streets of Huaycan where in some cases her scars help tell the stories captured in the songs she sings.

Together she and her children often work until late at night only to rise early the next day to do much of the same work all over again. What Maria is most proud of is the fact that, although she is quite behind in school fees, she has been able to keep most of her children in school. The reason she works so hard to provide her boys with an education is that she not only hopes to give them

more opportunities in life, but wishes to make them into much better men than the ones she has encountered in her life. She knows that she cannot change her past, but she can attempt to change the future and the type of men her young boys will grow up to be. It is an extremely difficult life she leads and but for the job she has created for herself, in what most people call the informal economy, she would not be able to take care of herself or her children at all. This is an example of how many of the world's poor create a living for themselves. It makes one think of that old adage "Necessity is the mother of invention." ■

Whether it is at the marketplace, far left, or on a bus, above, Maria Guzman often sings sad songs about her life. She sings for a largely captive audience who she hopes will care enough to help her and her children.

The Construction Women of India

Their ages vary along with their circumstances, but the goal of the millions upon millions of women throughout India who work with their hands and backs is often the same, and that is to provide support for their families so that the future lives of their children will look different from their own. Subadra Devi (40) looks as though she has worked all her life and has yet to find a moment to rest. She, along with a group of women, works alongside a road in Dharamsala, India. They work as manual laborers on a construction site. In this area of the world, the Himalayan foothills, construction workers often find work doing one of two things: either rebuilding roads that have collapsed down mountainsides as the result of the summer monsoons, which bring a deluge of rain to northern India, or building new homes or hotels for vacationers who escape to Dharamsala each year to find cleaner air and cooler temperatures than that found in India's central valley.

Ordinarily, construction work of this nature is not a job one would see many women attempting in the Western world, let alone dressed in brightly colored saris with nothing more than sandals on their feet. It is also not the job that any of these women saw themselves doing as children.

Nevertheless, life has offered them few options and today they work when and where they can. Many women who do this work are migrants and are among the poorest people in India. They travel throughout India searching for work as they go. Subadra herself left the state of Chhattisgarh in central India some years ago because of a drought that killed her crops. There was simply no work to be had in her community. It may not seem like their options now are much better, but at least they are able to work and support their families. It is because of their income that each of the women continues to hope for a life with some security, a home, and an education for her children. Of course, these women do not know if their dreams will ever be a reality, but finding and taking on as much work as they can helps keep the dreams alive.

Subadra remains determined to do everything in her power to change the future for her daughter. Her son, Sanjay (18), dropped out of school and is now working by her side. Subadra will take any work she can find but now fears that her son may end up as a laborer as well. Subadra says, "We have many dreams about the future but what can we do? This is our reality."

Subadra Devi, 40 (center), works at a construction site rebuilding a home and hillside that collapsed during a monsoon the previous summer in northern India. These women work very hard but make very little. When asked about her life Subadra said, "We have many dreams about our future but what can we do? This is our reality."

Anita Kumari (21), shown carrying rocks and gravel upon her head, helps Subadra mix rocks, cement, and gravel to build a retaining wall. It is work that is very hard on one's back. Anita brings her 3-year-old son, Girish, along with her while she works. He represents a constant reminder to her as to why she is there. She does not want her son to grow up to be a laborer because she knows how grueling this work can be. Anita also works digging ditches and stacking boulders alongside a road. The loads she places on her head weigh about 80 pounds, and she is by no means a large woman. For her work, she is paid an average of between 80 and 180 rupees a day (about $1.72 to $3.83 U.S.), and each day starts at 8:30 A.M. and ends at 7:00 P.M. Of course, too, at the end of her workday, she must attend to her home and family like the rest of the

Top left: It is in the face of Subadra Devi that we can see some of the signs of a hard life. It is work that her friend Anita Kumari, 21, bottom left and right (foreground), also does daily as she carries and hauls rocks in an effort to rebuild a retaining wall.

women working alongside her. It is a life of work, and it is work that clearly takes a toll on her body and her health. At the end of each day, she returns home incredibly sore from lifting boulders that in many places in the world would be done by heavy machinery but here is done by women.

Anita Kumari not only collects gravel but also hurls large stones to be used to hold back a mountainside, a mountain that often does not stay in place when the rains come. She and the other women work together and rent a local one-room shack for 400 rupees per month, or about $8.50 U.S. They dream of someday returning to their villages and building a house of their own but have never really found any kind of financial security as they do not have even a fixed workday. They also never know how long they will be needed on a construction site or what the work load will entail, and as a result they often do not know how much they might make on any given day. Nevertheless, they remain determined to provide their children with all they might need to escape the life they have before them.

Sharda Devi (30) works as a manual laborer in an area not far from where Subadra and Anita work. Her life is similar to the other women in many ways. She too works long days digging ditches, carrying bricks, and breaking down stones with a pick and shovel. But her life differs in one significant way: she has four children and her 12-year-old son, Rakesh, suffers from epilepsy. In order to care for her son, not only does half of her family's income go toward treatment and medication, but her oldest son, Vimod (15), must often work in construction as well. He no longer attends school because his income is also

needed to pay for his brother's health care. Sharda wants to be able to help Vimod finish his education, but she also hopes to continue to get Rakesh the treatment he needs in order for him to live a better life. And so she will continue to work at construction sites, as others do, and return home after a long day to care for all of her children.

The heat and the heavy lifting are enough to make even a large man feel the pain of the day, yet these women work right alongside men, showing they are capable of so much when working for a chance at a better future. How many could say they could walk a mile in these women's shoes and still have enough strength left to do it again, day after day? ∎

Far left: At another site not far from where Subadra works, Sharda Devi, 30, has labored for years in the hot sun with only sandals on her feet as one of her four children looks on. Above: These sandals offer little protection.

Left: Ana, 12, and Andrei, 8, are orphans and live in Chişinău, Moldova. Ana, like many big sisters throughout the world, has assumed the role of mother and cleans the homes of neighbors (above) in order to care for her brother. Often, instead of money they are given supper.

corporations have decided to have the labor associated with their products subcontracted abroad and pay individuals who live in developing countries much less than they would have to pay an equivalent labor force in their own country or the developed world. Companies that have gained some negative notoriety for their use of sweatshops have been Disney, Walmart, the Gap, and Nike. Nevertheless, because of the perceived need to produce products very inexpensively, maximize profits, and address the desire of many shoppers in the developed world to buy products at a low price, the proliferation of sweatshops around the world continues.

Millions upon millions of people around the world work in sweatshops, and sweatshops themselves can be found in nearly every country in the world. Those who work in sweatshops are mostly women, and most work for companies that make and sell apparel throughout the world. Although it is quite true that many sweatshops are located in some of the poorest countries in the

world, such as Vietnam, Jordan, India, Bangladesh, Honduras, Mexico, Indonesia, Swaziland, and South Africa, they are not always located in the very poorest countries. That is because large companies will not operate or place a plant in a country unless there is a reliable source of electricity, a stable government, and access to transport so they can move their products out of the country without too much difficulty or cost.

There are many advocacy groups and human rights organizations that have objected to the use of sweatshops because there have been simply too many problems associated with how the production of goods around the world have been managed by companies who often subcontract this work and provide little oversight to make sure that people are not exploited in one way or another. Some of these problems have included incidents where:

- migrant or trafficked workers were used at plants in situations where they were placed in fear that they would be reported to authorities or kept confined if they did not work long hours, take little or no pay, and do as they were told;
- workers were given absolutely no rights, no means to unionize, no compensation if injured at work, and no avenues to effectively pursue a grievance against a company;
- employers withheld pay or paid employees far less than they were promised;
- employees were forced to work long hours (thirteen-hour days) for seven days a week without any time off or much in the way of break time during the day;
- employees were forced to work with dangerous machinery or near toxic substances without any safety equipment;
- employees were forced to work in facilities that were poorly ventilated and prone to fires and, at the same time, could not take sick days without risking the loss of their jobs;
- children were being used as laborers in violation of child-labor laws;

Text continues on page 276

Two Lives, Two Factories

PARUL'S TWELVE-HOUR WORKDAY

Her name is Parul Begom (45), and she works in the city of Dhaka, the capital of Bangladesh, in one of the country's 3,000 plastic factories. She has one of the hardest jobs in the world and works long hours. Like many women who are poor and spend much of their lives working, she works for a specific employer and has to show up at a specific time to perform a specific task that she found in the formal labor market, but it is by no means easy. This is a truism that is clearly etched on her face.

Parul is the sole supporter of two of her four children and has for years been doing a job that brings her few, if any, rewards. She makes 650 taka a week (about $9.33 U.S.), a little over a dollar a day, for what are often twelve-hour workdays. To earn this money, Parul works all day gathering long plastic cables and feeds them into a hot molding press, which then melts and molds the plastic into smaller pieces. These pieces of plastic are then sold in the export market, which is one of the main exports of the country.

This is a job that is quite dangerous. Some time ago it caused Parul to lose part of her left hand. She severed her thumb when the hot molding press fell on it while shoving the plastic into the machine. It left her permanently maimed. The injury caused her to leave work for six months; during that time, however, and in as much as she had a specific employer and worked at a traditional factory, her employer did pay her so that she could continue to support herself and her family over the course of time she was away from work. It is hard to say whether this was part of the company's practice or just some kindness bestowed upon her by her employer, but certainly this practice is far more common when working for a large company.

Parul had to return to work because, to a large extent, it is the only work she knows and the only job available to her. She still experiences a great deal of pain as a result of her injury but continues to work to pay the rent of her small one-room metal dwelling perched atop a two-story structure, as well as pay for the care of her two children.

The pain that she lives with not only radiates from her hand but likely also has much to do with the fact that she is trapped among the fumes that surround her from the melting plastic that is

In the city of Dhaka, Bangladesh, there are many factories where millions of women work. Parul Begom, 45, is one such woman. She works twelve hours a day at a factory that recycles plastic wiring in debilitating heat for slightly more than a dollar a day.

produced from the machine she works on all day. The air is so thick with vapors it burns her eyes and causes her throat to seize. She has no mask to protect her from the elements that surround her and the fumes no doubt damage her body in far worse ways internally than do the obvious scars she has on her hands.

Parul's long day does not end when she leaves her place of employment. At that point, of course, she must go home to make sure her children have been fed and the needs of her small household have been taken care of. In the morning she rises at 7 to make some breakfast for herself and her children before she walks off to start another day alongside the machine that eats plastic. It is a job she dreads and a job that consumes one half of her life, but it is what she does to survive.

Left: Parul Begom's job requires her to feed plastic coated wiring into a machine that releases hazardous fumes as it chops the wire into recyclable pellets, sometimes taking a finger with it (top right). All this she endures in order to come home to a one-room metal enclosure to care for children (bottom right).

Mumtaz Hassanullah, 32 (far left, in purple), cuts thread with her teeth as she sews continuously in one of Bangladesh's many garment factories. It is a job she does from 8 A.M. to 8 P.M. nearly every day. These are long hours in an often hot environment which on average only pays her about 14 cents an hour, but it is work she accepts for it offers her at least a steady income, an income that she hopes to use to better the lives of her children. It is what is most important to her.

"I sew because my daughter wants to become a doctor and my son a policeman."

— Mumtaz Hassanullah (32)

A GARMENT FACTORY

Not far from where Parul lives and works we can find Mumtaz Hassanullah (32), sitting by a sewing machine in one of Bangladesh's garment factories. Many of these garment factories have been called sweatshops, for like many sweatshops throughout the world they are quite crowded, quite hot, and quite an ordeal for many who work there. Mumtaz works here in order to provide her children with the possibility of attaining their dreams. Her daughter, Rozina (12), wants to someday be a doctor while her son, Shuag (10), would like to become a policeman. Mumtaz values these dreams and works very hard so her children can continue to go to school and receive tutoring to keep up their grades and finish getting their education, an education Mumtaz believes will lead them out of their life of poverty.

Mumtaz starts her day at 6 A.M. and gets her children ready for school before she walks an hour to the garment factory where she works from 8 in the morning until 8 at night. It is a long, grueling day in a factory where many women such as herself work in harsh conditions making the clothes that so many of us in the Western world wear. For her

Left: At day's end, Mumtaz makes sure that her daughter, Rozina, 12, finishes her homework for she dreams of someday becoming a doctor.
Right: Mumtaz's husband, shown with their son, Shaug, 10, drives a rickshaw, and although they both make very little money, together they remain hopeful about the future and are seemingly happy.

labor Mumtaz makes about 14 cents U.S. an hour. It is hardly a fortune, but it is enough for Mumtaz to keep her children in school. In fact, when asked how she manages to keep her children in school, Mumtaz states that it is because she is able to work a significant number of hours each week. Hence, she believes that although her pay level is quite low it is the long hours that make it possible for her and her husband to lead a relatively reasonable life.

After work and on her way home, Mumtaz stops at the market to get food and then starts cooking dinner around 10 P.M. In the meantime her children work hard on their homework. Day in and day out Mumtaz must continue to work like this if she wants her children to have a better life. She knows she is better off than some, but it does not come easily. Her children wish they could do more to help her, but she refuses to allow them to do anything that distracts them from their schooling. She, like so many women around the world, is working for a cause bigger than herself and her own comfort.

On the rare occasion when you can find the whole of Mumtaz's family together, they often have huge smiles and are seemingly quite happy in the life they lead. Mumtaz's husband drives a rickshaw in and around the city of Dhaka, and together with his wife's income this helps keep their dreams alive. It may be one reason why they seem happy. ■

- employees were asked to live in overcrowded dormitories that were sometimes infested with vermin or bedbugs, and not adequately maintained or provided with clean water or private bathroom facilities;
- employees were abused by supervisors, sometimes sexually, and sometimes under threat of losing their jobs;
- employees were paid far less than they were entitled to and not enough to pay for the services sometimes provided by an employer, for example, food and shelter, and so they acquired much debt and continued to work as trapped, indentured servants.

By no means are these practices found in all sweatshops but, to the extent that they are, it is what makes that place of employment a sweatshop. In fact, although there is no universal definition of what makes a sweatshop, the U.S. Department of Labor defines a sweatshop as a factory that violates two or more labor laws, laws that often pertain to wages and benefits, child labor, and/or working hours. More generally, however, sweatshops can be defined as a workplace where workers are subject to exploitation including the absence of a living wage, benefits, poor working conditions, and arbitrary discipline including verbal or physical abuse. It does not matter whether companies are in the business of making apparel or other items such as electronics, tires, toys, shoes, rugs, auto parts, chocolate, coffee, or gathering and exporting bananas. A sweatshop can be anywhere, even in one's home.

In spite of all the problems that have been chronicled about the abuses associated with sweatshops throughout the world, many have argued, and probably not without a great deal of criticism, that the employment opportunities that have been provided to some of the world's poorest people in these large manufacturing plants have actually provided them with more good than harm. For the truth is that for the many who work in sweatshops in poor countries, their average monthly

---

FIVE THINGS TO KNOW ABOUT SWEATSHOPS

1. Sweatshops can be found in the United States. Usually they make apparel and are most likely to be found in the states of California, New York, Texas, Florida, and Georgia.

2. Within the apparel industry, approximately 85 percent of those who make clothing worldwide are young women between the ages of 15 and 25.

3. In most areas of the developing world the average pay for a sweatshop employee is between 15 and 50 cents U.S. per hour.

4. At the end of the day, employees at sweatshops in the developing world often spend from 50 percent to 75 percent of their income on food alone; many argue this makes it hard for them ever to escape poverty.

5. In the apparel industry, it is not uncommon for the people who made our garment to be paid less than 1 percent of its eventual cost at a retail store.

---

income is usually higher than the monthly income of a large percentage of the poorest people in their respective countries. For example, in Bangladesh, which has thousands of factories, over one third of all the people that live there make less than a dollar a day while those working in apparel factories make well over $1.50 U.S. a day despite the fact that in some cases they are paid as little as 14 cents an hour. This is true because the men and women who work at these plants usually work long hours, so even if they are paid a low hourly wage, far lower than one would expect they should rightfully receive, their overall income is substantially higher than a similarly situated person who might work for him- or herself and make less than a dollar a day, or on some days nothing at all. Bangladesh, by the way, has one of the lowest hourly pay rates for employees within this sector of work of any country in the world, although other countries such as Myanmar, China, Nicaragua, and Vietnam also pay very little.

Finally, sweatshop work is by no means the worst job in the world. As we noted in chapter 7 there are far worse ways to

Maria, 21, lives in Chișinău, Moldova, the poorest country in eastern Europe. Although she is a good worker and is often hired by her neighbors to work in their fields and gardens, she barely earns enough to provide for herself and her baby, which she supports on her own. It is a life that so many women around the world lead.

make a living. Many also argue that absent the jobs provided by these large manufacturing plants or call centers, people in these countries might otherwise be recycling garbage, crushing stones, farming for hours in the hot sun or rain, hustling on the street, pulling a rickshaw, or resorting to prostitution. Some economists have gone even further and said that the problem is not that we exploit too many of the world's poor in sweatshops, but that we don't exploit enough of them. Again, they believe that the work that many of the world's poor do in these factories has actually done much to lift them out of poverty in the same ways that immigrants in New York's Lower East Side eventually left that work, educated their children, and became a part of America's mainstream and middle class. To some extent the jobs that have been outsourced throughout the world have helped do the same thing for many. This, of course, cannot excuse the abuses that have occurred and continue to occur in the world's sweatshops, but it does shine a somewhat different light on the work that the poor do around the world. ■

CHAPTER NINE

And Yet the Children Play

If one were to travel throughout the world and ask many of those encountered who, of all the world's people, are least advantaged, I believe most would say children. Certainly there is a lot of truth to that, for few would disagree with the fact that among the world's people children have the least power to affect their lives, no political or economic power, and have little in the way of the physical strength necessary to protect themselves from the harm that the world often places in their path. Children also have little life experience and are perceived to have little wisdom, hence decisions that affect their lives are often taken from them and, for these as well as other reasons, they are essentially the most vulnerable among us. They rely on society's goodwill and their family and friends to raise, educate, and protect them. Unfortunately, in many cases and in many ways, their welfare is not furthered to the extent that it could or should be.

As evidence of this, one should know that:

- At present there are approximately 2.3 billion children in the world today. Children, as defined by international law, are persons under the age of 18. These children make up nearly one third of the world's population and, as mentioned above, have little or no power.

These three brothers are playing on a jungle gym at the Krousa Thmey Rescue Center in Phnom Penh, Cambodia. The center rescued the boys from a detention area after discovering that they had been forced by their parents to beg on the streets for money and were not attending school.

Children at Play

When one returns from visiting children all around the world, particularly children who are poor and have little, the image that one is left with is that children everywhere will always find a means to play. It seems an integral part of their nature, a way to simply be in touch with their inner self, a way to be free, and often a way to laugh and sometimes to forget the more sorrowful aspects of their lives.

Certainly children who are poor do not have the same kinds of instruments of play that more "advantaged" children have available to them. There are no Toys'R'Us, no Disney products, no video games, no games on their phones or in their bedrooms to fill their lives. Children who are poor make their own toys, create their own games, and simply play with things that they have found, made themselves, or inherited from a friend or relative. Sometimes, too, children live near natural play areas, for example, a wooded field where they can climb a tree or an old abandoned building that they can convert into a clubhouse or fort of one kind or another. Also-children will make playthings out of items not intended for play. For example, a mesh bag used to collect recyclables can be used by a child as a way to hide or scare friends as they

Although these children were seeking protection from the rain while keeping an eye on the cows they were herding in Nkwanta, Ghana, abandoned structures like this one often double as a clubhouse for children to play in all over the world.

Above: Here a little boy in Lima, Peru, plays peek-a-boo as he hides behind a mesh bag and peeks out at the world around him.
Far right: In far off Slatina, Romania, two young boys, like children everywhere, spar with sticks and pretend to be in battle over good and evil.

so much time to play. Something else that this movie seemed to suggest was that, in play, at least with this bottle, the children exercised such creativity that they learned much and creativity is certainly something that will prove useful to them in later life. So time is never wasted on play. It is all part of a child's learning process.

Other instruments of play that poor children often have at hand throughout the world are sticks. They can be found everywhere and often double as swords, or are balanced on top of a child's head, are used to hit rocks, or to draw pictures on the ground. Of all the toys that poor children seem to love the most, balls seem to bring the most satisfaction. Whether it be soccer balls or something akin to a baseball or bean bag, children are often content if even one ball enters their lives. When balls are not available, children sometimes turn to rocks to play with. They learn to throw rocks great distances or use them to play at games that involve target practice or as tools to dislodge fruit from trees.

In the tropics or in Southeast Asia, children can sometimes find vines hanging from trees, which they use like ropes and play jump rope. Whether they have seen this conduct elsewhere or invented it on their own, no one knows, but it is quite common and loved by children who have very little in the way of mass-produced toys.

For those children living near a waterway, there is always swimming or, better yet, diving. In some cases poor children are lucky enough to live near a waterfall and may decide to play there. Some play, of course, is quite dangerous and although there are no international figures as to how many children are injured or die as a result of the play they embark

play peek-a-boo through the openings in the mesh. There was a movie released in 1980 called *The Gods Must Be Crazy* that illustrates this point, in which a pilot of a small aircraft flies over the Kalahari Desert and, upon finishing a bottle of Coke, tosses it out the aircraft's window. The bottle proceeds to fall to earth and lands intact in a field near a village of San Bushmen in Botswana, Africa. The Bushmen quickly discover the bottle and decide to make use of it. Eventually, children who had never seen a bottle before fight over it because it was quite precious and they had devised many different ways in which to use the bottle as a toy. In some ways the children in this movie were blessed for it appeared that they had

Left: In Mae Sot, Thailand, some children have acquired a vine, which they use to play jump rope.

Top right: Two brothers in Nkwanta, Ghana, play with a ball they made themselves as they take a break from their work at weeding their father's farmland, while another child who lives close by (bottom right) practices balancing a stick as he gets through his day.

Left: In places such as Dhaka, Bangladesh, where water can be found, children often will take to swimming or diving as their play of choice, above, while on farmlands in Africa sometimes children simply resort to wrestling or horseplay.

upon, the figures are likely fairly high. Children in the developing world play in areas that are nowhere near as safe as a playground covered with tanbark or rubber matting, but then again this is just another by-product of poverty.

Other children who have few items in the way of toys will embark upon horseplay, the most common of which is wrestling with a parent, friend, or sibling. This kind of horseplay is healthy for it forms strong attachments and, unless, for some reason, it escalates into something else, it is often wonderful to watch.

Finally, there is always just that simple moment when children clap their hands, sing, and dance with a friend or sibling that brings so much

"Every child has the right to rest and leisure, to engage in play and recreational activities..."

— Article 3l, Convention on The Rights of the Child

joy to children who have so little. It is probably the most rudimentary type of play there is, so simple yet so fulfilling. The lesson gained from all of this is that play, and the opportunity to play, is something that all children seem to seek and even need. To live a life without play would probably create a great deal of stress in a child's life, for as we all know it is play and recreation that helps to relieve stress in all of us, and our children need that same kind of release. Many would argue that among all the sadness that exists in the world, a child who has never played, climbed a tree, run through a field, wrestled with a sibling, created a fantasy, or simply had a moment to sing and dance would be one of the saddest situations one could encounter. Thank God for the opportunity to play, and may all children, regardless of their circumstances, continue to be able to find a moment in their day to play. As mentioned, there now exists an international right to play. Hopefully, the adults of the world will learn to respect that right and see play as an essential part of the lives of children everywhere. For as to the children who have little else, play may be their only refuge. ∎

When children have absolutely no toys, for instance, these two children in New Delhi, India, they can always resort to singing and clapping their hands and in the process make each other laugh.

when the United Nations put forward and eventually put in place the Convention on the Rights of the Child. It is the most comprehensive international law ever created to foster and protect the rights, needs, and interests of children worldwide and has now been ratified by nearly all of the world's countries. Among many other aspects relevant to the lives of children, it seeks to protect the right of children to play. This right to play is embodied in Article 31 of the convention and contain words to the effect that:

1. "Every child has the right to rest and leisure, to engage in play and recreational activities appropriate to the age of the child and to participate freely in cultural life and the arts. [and]

2. "Member governments shall respect and promote the right of the child to participate fully in cultural and artistic life and shall encourage the provision of appropriate and equal opportunities for cultural, artistic, recreational and leisure activity."

The above restatement of Article 31 of the Convention on the Rights of the Child encompasses differing concepts, all motivated by the hope that children everywhere spend less time working and instead simply enjoy life. The concept of "play," however, as written into this document, seems to try to signify more than the simple meaning of play but rather suggests that play is intrinsic to childhood itself, a way of being that should not be controlled by adults, free from restraints and particularly open to a child's own creativity and imagination. This could be called "free play" and it is not a coincidence that free play is play that is most available to the children of the poor because it requires no special toys, expensive games, or playgrounds. It is an equal opportunity activity that nearly all children have access to and need in order to grow into healthy adults.

The Convention on the Rights of the Child also embodies many other articles that both directly and indirectly enhance a child's right to play. These articles include, but are not limited to:

Art. 12: The child's right to express his or her own views freely in all matters affecting the child

Art. 13: The child's right to freedom of expression

Art. 14: The right of the child to freedom of thought, conscience, and religion

Art. 15: The rights of the child to freedom of association and the freedom of peaceful assembly

Art. 29. The right of a child to an education directed to the development of the child's personality, talents, and mental and physical abilities. ■

It seems wherever there is an appropriate place, some time, and some children about, children will find a way to play. Here in the hills of Peru, three boys play a soccer game in an enclosure behind their home.

CHAPTER TEN

Hope

In this, the final chapter of the book, we should likely take a moment to apologize for some of the sadness associated with many of the stories and profiles we have highlighted throughout the previous pages. To be fair, we will still be doing a little more of that in this chapter, but for the most part, as we turn to the final pages of this book, we will try to present the positive. In other words, we will now turn to some of the progress and changes that have occurred in the recent past to relieve suffering on various fronts and which have improved the lives of millions of our global neighbors. Our hope also is to mention some of our upcoming challenges as well as outline some of the best thinking on how to bring an end to poverty and, while doing so, tell some stories of hope and change.

At the outset, however, it is very important for all to know that change is always possible and in fact is constant. It is part of life and is embodied in the natural order of things. When attempting to influence change in a positive direction (change that uplifts the world's condition and helps to relieve suffering) those who care must understand that while substantial positive change is often found in the cumulative actions of many, it does not mean that the millions, if not billions, of acts of kindness that occur around the world each day go without

At orphanages throughout the world, impoverished children receive meals that but for the existence of these orphanages children would simply go hungry. We owe much to these orphanages, such as this one in Peru, where children are blessed to be fed and now have a home.

notice, meaning, or value. Relevant here is a story told by Loren Eiseley called "The Star Thrower." It was first published in 1969 and it illustrates this point nicely. In short, and as later adapted from his work:

An old man had a habit of early morning walks on the beach. One day, after a storm, he saw a human figure in the distance moving like a dancer. As he came closer he saw that it was a young woman and she was not dancing but was reaching down to the sand, picking up starfish and very gently throwing them into the ocean.

"Young lady," he asked, *"Why are you throwing starfish into the ocean?"*

The young lady replied, *"The sun is up, and the tide is going out, and if I do not throw them in they will die."*

"But young lady," answered the old man, *"Do you not realize that there are miles and miles of beach and starfish all along it? You cannot possibly make a difference."*

The young woman listened politely, paused and then bent down, picked up another starfish and threw it into the sea, past the breaking waves, and while doing so replied, *"It made a difference for that one."*

The old man looked at the young woman inquisitively and thought about what she had done. Inspired, he joined her in throwing starfish back into the sea. Soon others joined, and all the starfish were saved.

The story of the starfish illustrates three points. First, that anyone and everyone can make a difference and that one person's actions need not be huge to be of worth. Although saving one starfish, one child, one family, or one village may not make a big difference in the world order, it does make a difference, in fact, a much bigger difference than if nothing was done at all. The second lesson learned by way of this story is that great change can grow out of the actions of one person. Jesus Christ,

Mahatma Gandhi, Martin Luther King, Jr., and Mother Teresa are all proof of that fact. Know, too, that kindness, compassion, and generosity are contagious and the good that people do for others everywhere is the rule, while greed and the desire for power is the exception.

The third lesson that one can take away from this story is that when an opportunity to do good comes along we should take advantage of that opportunity whether or not we are alone in our actions. Too often many of us wait for others to get involved or, worse, leave others to do what we should have rightfully attended to ourselves. Everyone's individual responsibility to do good should never be contingent on the actions of others. So remember, in our story of the starfish, the young woman was saving the starfish before the old man arrived and would have continued to do so even if he had walked away and never decided to help.

Of course, in addition to helping the world's poor, there exist many other difficult challenges that face the world today: challenges related to climate change and the warming of our earth, challenges related to the proliferation of nuclear weapons and war, the growing shortage of the world's resources, the need to improve the world's health care delivery systems and better combat future diseases or pandemics, and challenges related to the protection of human rights for all of the world's people. Add to this issues related to population growth and the migrations of populations, issues related to food and energy insecurity, and those related to the failings of some of the world's economic markets, and, yes, there are many challenges that lie before us. These challenges will require great ideas and the efforts of many, for the world today is more complex and more interdependent than ever before, and as a result these challenges will surely test all of us in the years to come. With this in mind, it is important to remain optimistic, since it is more true than not that it is the optimists of the world who often get the most done.

Ramina, 17, who lives in Moldova and was a victim of human trafficking, now carries her baby Ana, 9 months, outside for some sun. She works in a garden and is paid in food for her service. She lives in a small room with no electricity but occasionally has been able to borrow an electric line from neighbors. Each night she prays for the good health of her baby and food to eat. Luckily, she has received some help from a local group called Helen's Organization that specifically seeks to help young women like her.

Please keep in mind that if we look at the totality of the world's history, few would argue that we have not made great advances over some of our struggles of the past. To mention but a few, we have reduced the number of deaths that have occurred as a result of war and efforts at global conquests, we have reduced the percentage of those dying from various diseases and malnutrition, we have improved the world's overall standard of living, and, at least as of today, we have lowered the percentage of the world's population who live in abject poverty. All would

likely agree that with regard to the advancement and protection of human rights, the people of the world today, whether they be part of a marginalized group or not, have far more legal rights than ever before.

Some of the large-scale advances we have made have been the result of the concerted efforts of many individuals as well as world bodies such as the United Nations. Also, and in many cases, change was the result of social movements that had taken hold, lifted the consciousness of many, and moved us to change.

Text continues on page 314

Miguel Rodriguez:
A Story of Change and Hope

Miguel Rodriguez works in one of Peru's largest slums where he oversees the services provided by an orphanage he started years ago just outside the city of Lima. It has been over twenty years since the moment occurred that changed Miguel's life forever but, more important, it changed the lives of hundreds if not thousands of children.

Back in the late 1980s, Miguel had all the things that mirrored success: money, an education, a good job as a psychiatrist, a big house in a safe neighborhood, and a wife and three kids. These were the only things that mattered to him until a tragic day in Miguel's life changed his worldview.

On that day, his 6-month-old son, born with a heart defect, had a heart attack and the doctors at his local hospital could do nothing to save him. After watching his son die, Miguel ran out of the hospital. Upon leaving, however, he noticed two street children at the door of the hospital begging for medical help, but since they had no money they were not being admitted to the hospital. When Miguel saw these children, his first thought was that he wished God would have taken one of these children rather than his own. Miguel then saw his son's face in the faces of these two boys who were still alive and in need of

help. With that, Miguel paid for the boys' hospitalization and then walked home with his son in his arms. The next day, he returned to the hospital to visit with the boys, but by then one of them had died. Miguel felt this was a message to him, and that day he decided to do something to help the street children of Peru.

He began by taking his family to downtown Lima every afternoon to feed and bring medicine to the street children of the area. He started with thirty

Left: The children at La Sagrada Familia orphanage in a slum outside the city of Lima all come running when food is awaiting them. **Right:** Miguel Rodriguez, the beloved founder of this community, starts each day with a thank you to all those who continue to make this home possible for these children.

Above: At La Sagrada Familia, some of the 830 abandoned street children take time from what must be many worries to play soccer in a yard provided for them, while Miguel, far right, always takes a moment to greet every child as his own. It is his way of remembering a child he lost years ago.

garbage dumps, or working for unscrupulous people. Today, with the help of many others, he cares for some 830 abandoned street children from infancy to their adulthood at a home and center called La Sagrada Familia (the Sacred Family).

At his orphanage, he provides all his children with food, shelter, medical care, a formal education, employable skills, and, most important, a family. The children are responsible for cleaning their dorms and mud-brick shelters, bathing, doing laundry and other chores. They receive three meals a day and the older children help to care for the younger ones. There are also workshops offered that teach children carpentry, ceramics, sewing, music, and baking. Moreover, Miguel recently completed construction of a clinic on their grounds that will serve to generate an income for the settlement, because although the children and teachers will receive free medical care, the inhabitants in the surrounding community will be asked to pay for services provided to them.

Miguel, believing in the importance of play, a luxury that many of these children have never had, has also built a soccer court on the grounds of La Sagrada Familia where the children play in both the morning and late afternoon. The children, of course, use their play to forget about things they experienced on the street and some of the problems that life still has in store for them.

Miguel's greatest joy is simply walking around this community, visiting with the children, and giving as many as possible a hug and a word of encouragement. Each morning he makes an effort to greet every child at the orphanage with a kiss on the cheek, for he believes that no family is truly a family without the love and affection that families extend to one another. Miguel's family has gotten quite large and it has not

servings of food, which before too long grew to fifty servings and quickly he realized there were far too many children living on the streets. Shortly after, four small street boys asked if they could live with him. Miguel could not refuse and took them home and let them sleep in the room that once belonged to his son. Seeing that room once again filled with life and children safe in bed made him happy.

The next day the four children left, only to return that evening with eight more children. Miguel accepted them all into his home, only to later be accused by a neighbor of kidnapping the children. He sat in jail for three months before the authorities realized that he meant the children no harm. Instead of losing hope, however, Miguel reflected on his life and decided to sell his house and buy some land to start a home for street children. It started with a few children that he found living on the street, or in

always been easy for him to provide for them. On many occasions he wonders if there will be enough money to buy the rice and other food the children need each day. When food is short, he simply prays that someone will bring the food they need to feed the children. Miguel has said that it has never been easy, but his prayers have always been answered. By the end of the day, when all the children are in bed, he often takes a moment to simply sit on his couch and rejoice in the joy that La Sagrada Familia has brought to him.

Miguel's story and the building of his school and orphanage started with a decision to respond, to change something, even if that change, in the totality of things, was quite small. There are many millions of orphans and street children in the world and Miguel saves but a few. Nevertheless, the hope that was ignited by his decision to respond has spread to many lives. Because of one man the hope of these children was renewed, and today they have been given a chance at a productive life. In Miguel's words,

> "In all of us exists the hope of creating a new world. It's been twenty-one years since I came to believe in that world, to believe in humanity, to believe in God. But before, I did not. Before I believed in me. It was me first, me second, me third, me always.... Then my son died...I believe in new world now, a different world."

It is the real life stories of people like Miguel Rodriguez that should serve as a testament to the fact that we can all make a difference. Miguel started by bringing hope to one child and later to so many. We may take a different path, maybe tackle a different issue, but in doing so it's important to remember that in our own way we all have the ability to create a new world. ∎

With so many children and so much to do, every day at the orphanage is long. Nevertheless, by day's end, although exhausted, Miguel is always filled with joy, for few jobs are more rewarding than giving so many children a chance at a better life.

Krousa Thmey:
A Safe Place

Because of the overwhelming number of street children in the world, centers have sprung up in many countries that work to meet the immediate needs of children who have no place to go. As in the story of Miguel Rodriguez (previous profile), many of these centers were started by just one person who could no longer bear to walk by abandoned children and do nothing. Yes, it has been because of thousands of individuals who decided to begin the process of bringing some hope to millions of street children around the world that the lives of so many have been changed for the better. Often, however, these centers serve as just a temporary solution yet work to offer the children they serve some refuge from the harsh life they lead on the streets. At the Krousa Thmey (New Family) Center for Deprived Children in Phnom Penh, Cambodia, that is exactly what they try to do.

In Phnom Penh it has been estimated that on any given day there are about 20,000 children living and working on the city's streets, and although the Krousa Thmey Center has limited space for children on a long-term basis, most children there can stay only a short time. Nevertheless, this center tries to provide its

children with some time to sleep in a safe place, secure their few belongings, get some nourishment, bathe, play, attend school, and of course acquire some skills that might be useful to them on the streets of a big city. The center serves as a stopover point for most of the children that visit. It takes them in for a few months, and in addition to learning more about them, it tries to reintegrate them with their families. For a variety of reasons, that is not always possible. In some cases, returning these children to their families would not necessarily be in their best interest. So these children make do with what is given to them.

The center's school curriculum is made up of basic courses in mathematics, English, personal hygiene, singing, and dancing. To give one a sense of the kinds of children that Krousa Thmey rescues, consider five brothers who were brought to the center by a human rights worker. These boys had apparently been arrested for begging and were being held at a government detention center where they were not being given enough to eat. They were sent out on the streets by their parents and forced to beg after their parents lost their land because of a debt that had gone unpaid. At the Krousa

At the Krousa Thmey Center in Phnom Penh, Cambodia, five brothers sleep together on the floor. This is a temporary orphanage or, in reality, safe house for children who have been found abandoned and wandering the streets. Because space is limited, they cannot stay for long, but for now at least they are given some refuge from the influences of the streets of the city. These brothers range in age from 5 to 12.

Thmey Center they now receive food, shelter, clothing, and some schooling. The eldest, Boeun Sophorn (12), also takes a course in life skills so he can better protect and take care of his younger brothers Sophaif (11), Sopov (10), Sopheap (8), and Sammang (5). As this is only a temporary home for children, the center will try to help them find their family. If that is not possible they will have to be returned to the streets.

The children also have to participate in daily tasks such as cooking and cleaning. This is certainly not the best part of their day, but the children have to learn to be responsible for others and that when they work as a group it is then they can celebrate their accomplishments. Again, because of a lack resources, the children are free to leave this temporary shelter at any

At the center, children are fed, they receive some basic education and instruction in life skills, and are also put to work cooking and cleaning up after themselves. This builds their self-confidence and also gives them a better sense of family and the confidence to help one another.

"At the Krousa Thmey Center playtime is as important as everything else the children receive here."

— the staff of Krousa Thmey Center

time, but if and when they do the center tries to keep in contact with them, particularly those who are at greatest risk (young girls who may be seized and forced into prostitution and boys who are coerced to get involved in petty crimes or drugs). In order to try to do something about this problem, the center is now attempting to develop a system of family homes. These family homes are, in reality, a group of caring individuals that have offered their home to these children, giving priority to those who might most benefit from a homelike setting and have nowhere else to go. These families are trained and monitored by Krousa Thmey to make sure that the children are being well looked after and are attending school. For now, this is the best that the Krousa Thmey Center can do. It is an admirable effort at a problem that is global in nature, and the people involved are certainly making a difference in the lives of these children. ■

Although the children here appreciate everything, including time to play, life for them is quite basic, for the center has little funds and meals are sometimes just a cup of soup or rice. Nevertheless, it is the love and protection they receive here that is most important.

prepared food, but others at the marketplace were also selling fufu and the competition made the likelihood of making any profit through her labor nearly impossible. As the weeks went on and she was faced with the requirement to pay back her loan, Martha began to realize that she was actually in a worse position than she was before acquiring the loan. To help, her oldest grandchild, Luwis, traveled with her to the market and tried to sell water but rarely made any money at all. Martha had hoped that the micro loan might be the answer to her problems. Her dream was to make enough money to provide her grandchildren with medicine and food and possibly send at least one of them to school. Instead, she has been left with a product that does not sell and a loan that is seemingly impossible to pay back.

Martha's circumstances represent just one example of what happens when a micro loan is simply not the answer, at least if the money is to be used in the manner in which it was in her case. Martha also may not have been knowledgeable enough to do the market research necessary to come up with a good business plan, nor did she have the necessary skills to run a business. She also lives in an area where everyone is struggling and the economic conditions may not have not been suitable for any business. Martha and her three grandchildren are now also facing eviction, and the stress related to her new business can be seen on her face and the faces of her children, particularly now that Martha has to explain to the Foundation for Women that she will not be able to repay her loan.

It is situations such as Martha's that require us to reevaluate the micro financing system, and at a minimum be far more careful about the risks involved. It is important to understand why and when these loans work so we can better help the poor and those who are desperately looking for an answer to the very difficult circumstances life has brought them. Luckily, and after examining the bulk of the evidence that exists with regard to the effectiveness of micro lending worldwide, it seems clear that the system has done far more good for the world's poor than what the life of Martha Gbarpu would otherwise suggest. Nevertheless, we can always do better. ∎

Although micro loans have helped thousands, if not millions, throughout the world, Martha Gbarpu's business seems to be failing and may leave her and her grandchildren in a worse position than they had been in before they received their loan. This can be seen in both Martha's face, far left, and her granddaughter, Nohm, 5, above.

A final word about strategies that are used to try to help the world's poor: there is no silver bullet. Strategies that work in one place may not work in others. There are always too many variables. One needs to take time to assess the situation. No one wishes to invest resources in failed efforts. In fact, many believe that what is often needed to solve some regional problems are meetings with all stakeholders to discover what the obstacles to development have been and find out what efforts, if any, have taken place in the past. It is also sometimes helpful to speak to experts and then move slowly to test your development plan or project. Remember always to evaluate the work, plan for the long term, and eventually turn over what has been created to the community served so that the people can better help themselves.

A Word About Micro Lending

Everyone has heard about micro loans or micro financing. In short, micro loans provide the poor of the world with access to at least some funds to start a business or create for themselves an investment or income stream. To get these funds the poor have to apply, present a feasible business plan, and be willing and able to effectuate that plan. Loans are often less than $100 U.S. but recipients (or clients) can reapply as their business grows and needs increase. Sometimes these loans are needed to pay for a training program that might make it possible for one to acquire a skill and gain employment or become self-employed. More often, however, borrowers use the funds to start small shops off roadsides or in marketplaces. There they sometimes sell secondhand clothing, baskets, odds and ends, or street food of one kind or another in hopes of turning a profit and eventually finding a way out of poverty.

The truth is that the idea and availability of micro loans for the poor have been around for at least forty years. The person who has gotten the most credit for starting a system of micro loans worldwide is the Nobel Prize winner Muhammad Yunus.

Most of his work was done in Bangladesh, but now micro loans can be found throughout the world, with India likely making the greatest number of micro loans each year. It is now estimated that there are over a thousand micro financing institutions worldwide serving nearly 75 million borrowers who have taken out loans totaling nearly $40 billion. These institutions oversee small savings accounts for the poor with approximately $23 billion in deposits. Others have placed these numbers even higher, suggesting that there are now almost 700 million client accounts that have been opened around the world, intended primarily to serve the poor in the developing world. All, of course, started with two simple beliefs in mind: first, that the poor can be trusted to repay loans even if they have no collateral and, second, that the poor should be given the same opportunity to access credit as those who may be more privileged. Both ideas were first put into practice by Muhammad Yunus through his Grameen Bank.

It is hard to say anything negative about the work of these institutions in their efforts to help the world's poor. Over the years far more good than harm has been done through their efforts. Many millions have been able to start small businesses with the funds they have borrowed. Often these entrepreneurs are women who, but for these loans, would not have been able to escape poverty, support their children, or at least gain some independence and control over their own lives. Although there is some dispute over how many clients actually pay back their loans in full and on time, no one disputes that a much higher percentage of the poor do pay back their loans, and become eligible for new loans, than was originally envisioned by critics when such loans were first created. The poor have been a good investment.

There have been some problems associated with the making of micro loans, naturally enough. The truth is that we should almost expect that problems will occur when working in so many locales, with so many people, facing so many different kinds of obstacles just to survive. To be fair, some of the crit-

NAMASTE DIRECT

Namaste Direct works to help low-income businesswomen in the developing world acquire the tools necessary to improve their businesses in order that they might move from semi-poverty toward the middle class. This will promote the well-being of women and their families, community development, and participatory democracy.

Address: 1408 Hudson Avenue
San Francisco, CA 94124
Phone: (415) 440-2228
Email: info@namastedirect.org
Website: www.namastedirect.org

THE ONE CAMPAIGN

The One Campaign is a grassroots advocacy and campaigning organization that fights extreme poverty and preventable disease, particularly in Africa, by raising public awareness and pressuring political leaders to support smart and effective policies and programs that are saving lives, helping to put kids in school, and improving futures. Cofounded by singer and activist Bono, ONE is nonpartisan and works closely with African activists and policy makers.

Address: 1400 I St., NW Suite 600
Washington, DC 20005
Phone: (202) 495-2700
Email: Form online
Website: www.one.org/us

PARTNERS IN HEALTH

Partners in Health has developed a model of community-based health care that it uses in twelve countries across the globe. And by doing so PIH has been driven by three goals: to care for patients, to alleviate the root causes of disease, and to share lessons learned with other countries and NGOs. Partners in Health brings the benefits of modern medicine to those most in need and works to alleviate the crushing economic and social burdens of poverty that exacerbate disease.

Address: 888 Commonwealth Avenue, 3rd Flr
Boston, MA 02215
Phone: (617) 998-8922
Email: info@pih.org
Website: www.pih.org

PLAN USA

Plan USA works side by side with communities in fifty developing countries to end the cycle of poverty for children. Its vision is of a world in which all children realize their full potential in societies that respect people's rights and dignity. Its program also strives to achieve lasting improvements in the quality of life of vulnerable children in developing countries by enabling children, their families, and their communities to meet basic needs and to increase their ability to participate in, and benefit from, their societies; fostering relationships to increase understanding and unity among peoples of different cultures and countries; and promoting the rights and interests of the world's children.

Address: 155 Plan Way
Warwick, RI 02886
Phone: (800) 556-7918
Email: Online form
Website: www.planusa.org

WORLD PULSE

World Pulse's mission is to lift and unite women's voices. With a focus on grassroots change, its programs nurture community, provide media and empowerment training, and channel rising voices to influential forums. Today women from nearly every country in the world use World Pulse to speak out and connect, using Internet cafés and cell phones from rural villages to urban cities. By networking on its website, women are finding jobs, starting new programs and businesses, launching women-only cyber cafés, and finding international speaking opportunities that are changing their lives and the world.

Address: 1006 SE Grand Avenue, Suite 200
Portland, OR 97214
Phone: (503) 331-3900
Email: Form online
Website: www.worldpulse.com

ZIDISHA

Zidisha is a peer-to-peer microlending service offering direct interaction between borrowers and lenders across the international wealth divide.

Address: 21900 Muirfield Circle, 302
Sterling, VA 20164
Phone: N/A
Email: service@zidisha.org
Website: www.zidisha.org

Afterword

People are dying. People are suffering for no reason.

There are enough resources in this world for everyone.

Why does this problem still exist?

Even after traveling the globe, visiting ten countries on four continents to put human faces on the issue of global poverty, I cannot fully answer that question. But I did learn one extraordinary truth: the human spirit transcends even the worst deprivation. And if we hope to change it we must connect at that most human level.

I witnessed people suffering from the ravages of war, disease, child labor, forced prostitution, starvation, rape, homelessness, abandonment, blindness, and environmental toxins with little or no hope of help.

In Liberia, barbed-wire fences and huge billboards that said "Real Men Don't Rape" were a constant reminder of the previous war and its aftermath. I found children as young as eight years old who had lost their families in the war, had been raped, and were living in an orphanage that was ill equipped for healthy children, much less those who had suffered such emotional trauma. They had little food, scant shelter, and no supplies. One girl, suffering from a fistula, had soaked her mattress and was sleeping on just the metal springs of the bed frame.

Of all the things I witnessed while working on this project, these are the faces that are etched in my memory forever. Amazingly these children didn't ask for food or even a home. All that these innocent victims of horror wanted were supplies so they could attend school.

In India, I photographed a 22-year-old mother who was starving her child so she could use her to beg on the streets to earn money to feed her other children. The child was two years old and weighed nine pounds.

Sacrificing one child to feed your others is almost unimaginable. This photograph is so searing that I fear you will dismiss it as something alien, something so outside your experience that it doesn't feel real.

I'm asking you not to turn the page quickly. Look, really look, at these faces. Imagine yourself behind these eyes. For without that connection this project is lost.

When I was a little girl I would imagine myself escaping into the frame of a wonderful impressionist painting at the Metropolitan Museum of Art in New York City. I would immerse myself in the pastoral beauty among the flowers and landscapes that captured my heart.

I never imagined myself in the grim world of 8-year-old Fati, tears streaming down her face from the effects of malaria while balancing a bucket on her head, as she scavenged through toxic e-waste barely able to breathe in the hope of finding something to sell to survive.

I'm asking you to immerse yourself in these photographs as if this were your reality. Could you survive with no home, not even a mattress? Breathing the black soot of toxic waste? Drinking contaminated water? Walking miles and days just to find water or food? Facing starvation? Enduring head-splitting pain from malaria with no hope of medicine or treatment, ever? Being sold into prostitution by your family and forced to have sex day in and day out as your eyes turn yellow from hepatitis? Running in the African bush, terrified of being blinded by a snake bite, from sunrise to sunset as the four small boys I photographed in Ghana did every day?

It's a hard reality to face, never mind try and fix. But if we cannot connect, cannot imagine, cannot see, we can never hope to change.

For me, just as it did in the Met, my heart led me to our shared humanity, inspired by the dignity, love, and even laughter against all odds that I witnessed.

Text by Thomas A. Nazario © 2013

Foreword by the The 14th Dalai Lama © 2013

Photographs by Renée C. Byer © 2013

Printed in China
Manufacturing through Asia-Pacific Offset, China

Library of Congress Cataloging-in-Publication Data

Nazario, Thomas A.

Living on a dollar a day : the lives and faces of the world's poor / by Thomas A. Nazario ; photos by Renée C. Byer ; foreword by The 14th Dalai Lama.

    pages cm

ISBN 978-1-59372-056-8

1. Poor. 2. Poverty. 3. Rural poor. 4. Poor children. 5. Equality. I. Title.

HC79.P6.N39 2013

305.5'69--dc23

2013033247

The Quantuck Lane Press, New York
www.quantucklanepress.com

Distributed by W. W. Norton & Company, 500 Fifth Avenue, New York, NY 10110
www.wwnorton.com

W. W. Norton & Company Ltd., Castle House, 75/76 Wells Street, London, W1T 3QT

1 2 3 4 5 6 7 8 9 0

The Forgotten International works to bring people in the world who have great resources together with people who have great needs in order to help alleviate poverty, particularly that experienced by women and children, both in the United States and worldwide. Through these partnerships, those in need are given the gift of hope, while those who help are given the gift of knowing that the world has been made better through their kindness and compassion.

The Forgotten International operates entirely on donations and focuses its limited resources within four main program areas. We provide mini grants to trusted community organizations, village schools, charitable medical clinics, and orphanages that make the most of all their resources. A Fellowship Program whereby we send skilled volunteers to live and work abroad with grassroots organizations that directly serve the impoverished members of their local communities. A materials donation program where, in collaboration with our partners, we send donated goods and supplies to communities in need around the world, and finally, we work to raise awareness of the problem of global poverty through community presentations, videos of our programs, our publications, and our Compassion Education Project.

If you would like to learn more about us or get involved in our work, please feel free to contact us.

The Forgotten International

P.O. Box 192066
San Francisco, California 94119 USA

415-517-6942

info@theforgottenintl.org

www.theforgottenintl.org